START
GOLF
YOUNG

Doug Ford in a typical swing.

The shot that went down in golfing history was made by the author on April 7, 1957, when he was a shot behind in the Masters Tournament in Augusta, Georgia, and his approach shot to the 18th green landed in a sand trap. With a sand blaster he exploded out—right into the cup—for a birdie and a score of 66 to win the tournament.

DOUG FORD

START GOLF YOUNG

STERLING PUBLISHING CO., INC. NEW YORK

Oak Tree Press Co., Ltd. London & Sydney

OTHER SPORTS BOOKS OF INTEREST

Getting Started in Tennis   Junior Karate
Girls' Basketball   Junior Tennis
Girls' Gymnastics   Karate for Young People
Golf Explained   Kung Fu for Young People
Junior Judo   Warm Up for Little League Baseball

ACKNOWLEDGMENTS

The glossary for this book was taken in large part from "Golf Explained," © 1977 by Peter Dobereiner, published by Sterling.

Contents

You Are Shooting . . . How to Stand . . . Hands and Head at Address . . . How to Grip the Club . . . The Backswing . . . The Top of Your Swing . . . The Downswing . . . Point of Impact . . . How to Follow Through . . . Practicing Your Swing

1. Why Play Golf?

When you were very young, you probably dreamed of becoming a baseball or softball hero. You may have thought of football in the fall, or basketball in the winter, but the spring was baseball time. Today, the average sports-minded American boy or girl grows up thinking of golf as a spring sport as much as of baseball. Older people, past adolescence, leading sedentary lives and not getting enough exercise, are turning to golf more and more. Why is this?

Where baseball and football and basketball require a team—in fact, two teams!—you can play golf solo; or with one companion, or two or three. Then too, unlike the team games which become too strenuous for people over 40 (perhaps even over 35), golf lasts a lifetime. You can get just as much satisfaction from golf at 70 as you can in your teens.

What else is in back of the steady increase in popularity of golf? I'm inclined to attribute some credit to the colleges for the surge of new young golfers. It is college golfers and TV coverage of tournaments that have given the game an added impetus.

When I was a youngster Bobby Jones was my hero. Even at the tender age of 14 he had been a whiz of a golfer, and as he took championship after championship he captured the attention of people the world over. In more recent years, Arnold Palmer and Jack Nicklaus have done the same thing. The spectacular feats of these men and others like them in the pro ranks have brought the game of golf to the attention of millions of sports fans, including youngsters.

GOLF IS AVAILABLE TO ALL

At one time, not so long ago, golf was thought of as a rich man's game. When a man reached the age of 40 he joined a country club, where his family sat on the veranda while he took golf lessons. By the time he was able to pick his way around the 18 holes, he had met a group of similar duffers, all businessmen with a bit of money who had similar ideas. He worked out business deals on the golf course, and his family got into a higher bracket of society. Undoubtedly some of this goes on even today. But golf is no longer just a rich man's game and it isn't strictly a country club phenomenon.

My own upbringing was on a public golf course. Today there are more public courses than ever before. There are beautiful courses being built in vacation spots and in the suburban areas outside all major cities. Those that were built years ago have never been so popular. In the more rural areas, golf courses have replaced many a hayfield, and 9-hole courses dot the countryside wherever you look. The exclusive country clubs no longer have a monopoly on the game. This means that if you want to play golf you can find yourself a nearby course where, for a small fee, you can play a round of golf.

THE PLEASURES OF GOLF

The reason that most people take up the game—and stick to it—is because golf is fun to play! If it weren't a *pleasure* to sock a tiny white pellet around a rolling green landscape (comedians' "jokes" notwithstanding), you and I wouldn't be golfers. As it is, I would play golf for pleasure if I weren't a professional. No matter what kind of life you lead—whether you go to elementary or high school or college, whether you are a stenographer or an executive, a factory hand or an aviator—just go out on a driving range and hit a few balls. Once you have hit a golf ball just right, and feel that warm surge of pleasure creep from your toes right up the back of your neck, you probably won't be able to resist the temptation to get out on a golf course at every opportunity.

That's an important point about golf. You're not only in competition with your fellow players, but you're stacking your skill against the score card, against the course itself. The trees are a handicap you have to fly over, or get around somehow. The sand lies in wait if you stray from the straight and narrow fairway. The high grass is ready to hide your ball from sight. The smooth green acts like an icy lake when your ball bounces on it without backspin. All the beautiful objects of nature, which you can admire as you walk around, turn into gigantic gargoyles if you don't watch out!

That brings us to another competitor when you play golf—yourself. It's fun to test yourself, to train yourself to a discipline that only you are aware of. I can't even express the pleasure I get out of knowing that my muscles are trained to swing just the right way to send the ball flying directly on a line to the pin. When I break a 72-par by 6 strokes I have conquered *myself*, whether or not someone else has shot 7 under par. I have won first place in 19 tour events, including the PGA Championship, the Masters, and the Canadian Open twice. If I don't win top money in a tournament, I can still thrill to the fact that I came close. If I can control myself just a little better next year and the year after that, I may win more prizes and that will give me still more pleasure.

I'm simply pointing out that even a professional golfer, who might be thought of as a businessman-on-the-links, is truly a "player" at this game more than a "worker." I'm not the only one. All my fellow pros feel the same way, I'm sure. The pro who takes his game too seriously cannot last long. It's a game, a sport, and only incidentally can one make money at it.

GOLF IS MUSCLE-BUILDING

No other game is as healthful as golf! I know that's going out on a limb, but I'm prepared to back up that statement with facts.

If a game is judged by the number of skills it requires and the number of muscles of the body that are used, then golf is the leader. It's said that in swimming you use every muscle of your body. In golf, you use not only every muscle, but your eyes and brains as well. If you play golf regularly, your arms and shoulders will become as strong as a baseball player's. Your legs and ankles will become as supple and strong as a football player's. Your lungs will fill with the ozone from the tree-filled landscape. Your skin will feel the stimulation of the sun's rays. Your heart won't be taxed by running, or your bones broken by tackles or slides, or your fingers split by catching a ball. I can't remember the last time a pro golfer was injured on a golf course!

Naturally, if you take chances and break the rules of golf etiquette, you may get hit by a golf ball, and that's no pleasure. But, when you're health-minded, you're also courtesy-minded, and you won't take chances.

If you have a bad leg or arm, golf is probably one of the few games you *can* play. Ed Furgol didn't allow a withered arm to prevent him from becoming U.S. Open Champion in 1954. Thousands of players, and good ones, have one or another physical handicap.

You don't have to be big or strong to be a good golfer! Size doesn't matter a bit. Ben Crenshaw, a Young Lion, weighs about 135 lbs. (61 kilos), and Tom Watson isn't much heavier. Rod Curl is just over 5 feet (150 cm), and you won't find a fiercer competitor anywhere in any sport. Golf is not a game of brute force, as football is. It doesn't give advantages to extremely tall players, as basketball does. You don't have to

11

have the physical endurance to stand in the same square under a blistering sun all afternoon, as a tennis player does. You don't have to resist a chill, as a swimmer does.

If you're just an average size fellow, or girl, and you want to be comfortable and enjoy a sport that doesn't overtax your strength, golf is the game for you! While you're having fun, gradually and slowly you will be developing muscles you didn't even know were there, and bringing out skills you didn't know you had.

WHY YOU SHOULD START NOW

Psychologists tell us that the younger you are, the faster you learn, and the older you are, the more you know. I found this out for myself. I can teach a certain amount of golf in 20 minutes to a teen-ager, and it takes me perhaps 20 days to teach the same amount to a person over 35; the youngster will quickly forget a good many of the things that he's learned and the older person will remember them all. The older you get, the harder it becomes to teach your muscles the discipline necessary for golf. Your brain learns but your muscles are too set to learn rapidly after you are past your 20's. This means, then, that the older man or woman has to study harder and practice more. The younger person has to remember better.

The ideal time to learn golf is while you're still in your teens or even younger. My son, Doug, learned to play a pretty good game of golf at the age of 9. He had specially-built clubs. Today, special-size clubs for youngsters can be bought at practically any golf shop. I learned to play when I was in my teens. While you're that young, you probably have the time to get out several afternoons a week after school.

Judy Rankin, one of the all-time career money winners in women's golf, started playing golf at age 6, started winning championships at age 8, became the youngest-ever Missouri state champion at age 14, and at the age of 17 became a professional, one of the youngest ever to join the **LPGA** (Ladies Professional Golf Association) tour.

You can't find as much time to play golf when you're working in an office. Weekends are fine for playing and at least two rounds a week are almost essential during your beginning years. You have to depend on Saturdays and Sundays and pray that it won't rain one of those days. (All right, you can play in the rain, but that will only help your game if you turn professional.)

Is learning from a professional better than learning from a book? Certainly it is, but you learn different things. The next best thing to taking personal lessons is studying a book such as this, learning the rules and purposes of the game. If you know the rules and you know what you're supposed to do, then the professional teacher can watch to see that you do it. He has a better basis on which to add his personal teaching.

The youngster, too, must learn the rules and purposes of the game and show serious intent by studying and remembering.

While you're young, you can caddy. Even older beginners can caddy—not as a regular thing, but on occasion. Don't scoff at this. Most of the top golfers have been caddies, not only because they needed the money, but because it gave them a way of learning golf and getting golf under their skin. The familiarity they obtained with all kinds of golfers, good and bad, and all kinds of situations stood them in good stead.

Caddies have a chance to swing all kinds of clubs. You'll see them on the course, waiting for their "man" to tee off, trying every club in the bag, discovering an old cleek, or a fancy-headed putter, or an old wood shaft. They see duffers make the worst mistakes and land in the most difficult situations. I don't say that a caddie can learn more from a duffer than a pro, but he certainly will cover more ground and see more unusual recovery shots.

A youngster who caddies quickly learns which players make the good shots and low scores, and which are the hopeless ones. From that, it's an easy step to figure out which swings are good and which are bad. After a month or so of caddying, you can figure that you've had the equivalent of one year of expert instruction. Caddie scholarships are available to candidates of proven character and academic achievement. See page 137 for a sample scholarship fund. Golf schools are also available for those young golfers who wish to further develop their skills and improve their game. For a directory of golf schools in the U.S. and assistance in choosing one, see pages 127 to 134.

Of the famous golfers who attribute their success to their college golfing days count Tom Watson, Jack Nicklaus and Arnold Palmer, to name just a few. Most of them became great without ever having had a single formal golf lesson.

HOW I STARTED

My father was a professional golfer. He had a driving range a few blocks from our home on a lot under the Broadway elevated line near Van Cortlandt Park in New York City. In bad weather and in winter, he moved his business into an indoor school.

Whenever I had the chance, I went over to the driving range. It was there that I found out what a pleasure golf is—even on a big city driving range.

At just about this time, while I was going to high school in New York's Washington Heights, I was tempted by baseball. Buddy Kerr, who later became the Giants' best fielding shortstop, was a friend of mine at high school. I played a pretty nifty third base. Baseball was a big thing in my neighborhood. The kids played stickball in the streets, and I had been a star at that. So, one day when Buddy Kerr was invited by the Yankees to come over to the Stadium and talk about a baseball contract, I went along with him and some other boys.

We saw the Yankees scout, Paul Kritchell, and we talked about D Leagues. Buddy was interested, and so was I, but no offer was forthcoming that day, and I never went back to follow up on the conversation. I'm glad now I didn't. Before long, I forgot all about baseball and became wrapped up in golf.

High school was out for the summer, and Van Cortlandt Park's public golf course wasn't very far away—in fact, it was within walking distance. That course became my home for the summer, and my home after school when fall came.

The fees were modest, and I was easily able to afford a season ticket. However, the course wasn't top-notch. It consisted of 12 flat holes and 6 "hill-holes." The flat holes were fairly long, but the greens were not well-trapped, and there were practically no difficult shots, except for one water hole. You had to go over a circular pond from tee to green, a distance of about 135 yards (122 m), as I recall. That was the first hazard hole I learned to play. The hill holes were more challenging, but they were short. If you had a little mountain-goat blood in your veins, you could navigate the hills fairly easily. Coming downhill was a cinch, and it was on the sharp slopes that I learned how to put backspin on a ball.

The nearby public course of Mosholu was shorter and easier, so when I became a little more proficient, I had to find more difficult courses. Finally, after some cooperation from my father, who had been instructing me all along, I graduated to membership in a country club in Westchester County. Then I could enter amateur tournaments—and I did.

I won the New York State Amateur title in 1940 and 1941, while still in my teens. Then I went into the Coast Guard in 1942. After the war, I went back to amateur tournaments, and in 1949 I turned pro. I've played what the pros call the "winter circuit" and the "summer circuit" and in between times I've taught golf—1978 will be my 29th year competing

15

on the TPD (Tournament Players Division) tour. I've enjoyed every minute of my career, and I expect to continue enjoying myself.

WHAT TO EXPECT FROM GOLF

If you take my advice and start now, don't expect to burn up the course right away. You'll probably start out like everyone else, shooting somewhere between 100 and 130 for 18 holes. After a month or so, you should begin to think about breaking 100. If you're a girl, add about 10 strokes to those scores. If you have average ability and play at least two days a week, you should be shooting in the 90's within a year.

From there on, you'll need better than average ability. *If you have it,* it's just a step to the middle 80's and that's where real championship class should begin to tell.

If you can shoot below 85 *consistently* after a couple of years, you're slated to be a fine golfer. If you then take enough interest in the game, and apply yourself to mastering the little things that knock strokes off your score bit by bit, you're headed for championship rank and low-70 consistency. When I was 16, I was shooting 72 or 73 quite often on my first full-length courses. That indicated I had a natural aptitude for the game and it prompted me to stick with it for a livelihood.

You will not get as much satisfaction from golf if you remain a duffer all your life—don't let anyone kid you. You have to play a pretty good game (somewhere below 100) to be happy for any length of time. So you should learn as much as you can at the start. Learn, practice, remember. Learn more, practice, remember. That's the cycle that takes you out of the duffer class into the "expert" class, if not into the pro class.

That's the reason for this book—to make it easy for you to learn the things that a book can teach you, so you won't have to waste time learning them out on the course, and so you can spend that time outdoors practicing and becoming perfect.

After you've learned the game thoroughly, you'll thank your lucky stars time and time again throughout your life that you started this wonderful, fascinating, healthful and rewarding game.

2. How a Course Is Laid Out

Before you learn to swing a club or hit a golf ball, it's a good idea to know what the purpose of the game is and what a golf course really is.

You may know that the purpose of the game is to hit a golf ball around the 18 holes of the course in the *lowest* possible number of strokes. You must start on the tee of each hole and hit the ball with one club or another (not touching it with your hands or body once you've teed up) until you've stroked it into the cup of that hole. You add up the number of strokes you take on each hole to get your total score for the 18. That's simple enough. (You'll find a discussion of the rules of golf on pages 107 to 119.)

What are the 18 holes like? Are they the same on each course? No, they're very different, and that makes it interesting to play different courses, but it also makes it difficult. A pro in a tournament at a new course is under a handicap, as against a player who knows the course thoroughly. By the same token, the average amateur should be able to save 5 strokes in 100 simply by knowing the course he's playing.

Some golfers have been playing for years without ever thinking about how best to play a course. You'll be a better golfer if you know a few important essentials that apply to all kinds of golf courses.

WHAT PAR MEANS

You can only play one hole at a time. I mean this not only literally. I mean that you should concentrate on the hole you're playing, and not think about the hole you just played or the one that comes next.

Each hole has a "par" value, and a course has a total par—usually 70, 71 or 72, for the 18 holes. This is quite different from the par value of stocks and bonds. In golf, par is the number of strokes assigned to each hole for the *faultless play* of that hole. Actually, when a golfer plays a hole under par (as you will, too), he is playing "better than faultlessly."

The par of each hole in America has been assigned to it by a club committee working under the recommendations of the United States Golf Association. The committee is concerned with the *length* of the hole and not its difficulty.

How does this work? By rule, any hole up to 250 yards (225 m) from tee to cup can be a par-3. If the hole is uphill or twisting, or over rocks, or somehow especially difficult, and close to 250 yards (225 m) long, the committee may assign a par-4 to it. On the other hand, if a hole is only 100 yards (90 m) long, it's still a par-3. There is no par less than a 3-par.

Why? Because "faultless play" in putting (on the green) is considered to be 2 strokes. On each and every green, you're allowed 2 putts, according to the par-assignment committee. Naturally, you want to get your ball in the cup with 1 putt, and many times you can and will. If you're a good putter you'll have a good chance of breaking par—it's as simple as that—if you can get *on the green* in the par-number of strokes. On a par-3 hole, you're allowed one shot to get on the green and 2 putts to get in.

Par-4 holes are supposed to run from 251 yards to 475 yards (226 to 428 m), but as we've seen they may be shorter under special circumstances. It is seldom that a hole of less than 480 yards (432 m) is assigned a par-5. The longer holes of 480 yards (432 m) and longer are either par-5 or par-6. Technically, a par-6 can be assigned to a hole of 600 yards (540 m) and more, but there are few holes as long as this. I know of only one. Par-6 holes are too easy to get birdies on (one stroke under par is called a "birdie" and two under par an "eagle").

PAR-5 HOLES

The long holes are the easy ones for a good golfer. It is possible to hit a ball with a driver 250 yards (225 m) without too much trouble, and follow up with a 3-wood shot of equal length. That's 500 yards (450 m). If the green of a par-5 hole is 500 yards (450 m) from the tee, you may easily get on the green in 2 long shots. Then if you get down in the regulation 2 putts you have a birdie. If you sink your first putt you have an eagle. Surprised? Try it. In your early days of golf, concentrate on chopping off strokes on the long holes, and play the short holes carefully.

PAR-3 HOLES

Usually the holes that you can reach with a driver or with an iron have obstacles that trick you. The green may slant toward the tee or off to one side, so that the ball rolls off when it hits (unless you can control it). Or there may be heavy woods on each side of the green with only a narrow path to hit through. Or the green may be on an island completely surrounded by water or sand traps. Golf course architects have a way of thinking up the most beautiful tricks for the placing of greens on the short holes. The more par-3 holes a course has the harder it is. So play them safe.

TEES AND WHAT THEY'RE FOR

What do I mean by "safe" when a hole is difficult?

Safety consists of taking every advantage of the rules. For instance, every hole has a "tee." I'm not now speaking of the little wooden (or plastic or rubber) peg you insert in the ground to place your ball on. I'm referring to the teeing area, the square or oblong place which is marked off somehow as the place on a hole to start. There are usually two markers set in a line to show you where to start.

Now, some golfers like to show off. They tee up way in back of the line for no other reason than to be dramatic. Don't be like that. Tee up as near the green as you're allowed. (The only time you tee up farther back is when you can't otherwise find a firm spot to get a stance.) Nobody can or will criticize you for following the rules to a "t," especially on the tee and with a tee. That brings up another point.

Always use a tee (the peg)—even on a short hole where you tee off with an iron instead of a wood club. The teeing up of your ball allows you to hit it without touching the ground. The grass can and sometimes does deflect your clubhead and prevent you from hitting the ball straight. Here, avoiding trouble is a safety measure: the little peg can't deflect your club! The rules allow you to tee up the ball on every tee, and nowhere else. Take advantage of this.

Some duffers claim that they can get backspin more easily when they play the ball from grass instead of from a tee. This is just something they've talked themselves into. If you hit down on the ball with your pitching iron, you'll get plenty of backspin off the tee, as you'll learn in the chapter on short iron play. You'll get fewer "flyers" (balls hit out of control) when you don't let the grass interfere, and you'll get better distance more easily when you tee up on a short hole.

Of course, when you use a wood club for a drive always tee up the ball. Tee up where the grass is short and the ground is firm for your feet.

You have the choice of hitting from the left or right side of the tee, or from the middle. If you have an obstacle to get around or over, and teeing up on one side of the tee will help you, by all means do it.

If the hole is a dog-leg to the left (that is, the fairway turns to the left some yards out), you'll have a better chance of landing on the fairway with a straight drive if you tee up on the right side of the tee. See why? A straight drive from the left of the tee may carry you right across the fairway and land you in the woods. A hooked drive (pulled to the left) will land you in the woods and so will a sliced drive (pushed to the right). From the right of the tee, a hooked drive may be just what you want; a sliced drive will land you in trouble in any case. The straight drive has more fairway ahead of it to roll on.

(Talking about a dog-leg, play the hole as it is designed. Don't try to cut a corner by going over the high trees. That's showing off in a beginner. The pros will only cut corners if the wind is favorable to them, and will give them a better than 75 per cent chance of picking up *a stroke*, not just yardage. A pro who is far behind in a tournament may take that chance with lesser odds because without it he has lost. Under ordinary circumstances, however, playing safe is always the best policy.)

There are other occasions too when you don't tee in the center. If there is a strong cross-wind, for instance, you have to take that into consideration. If there are traps on one side of the fairway or another, tee to hit away from them. Or if the fairway slopes to one side, you want to play along the topside of the hill to get the longest possible roll.

Once you're off the tee, there's nothing you can do about the position of your ball. You have to play the ball from where it lies. If it lies on the fairway on close-cropped grass—fine! You'll have a good chance for a clean second shot.

FAIRWAYS SHOW THE WAY

According to golf course regulations, a fairway (the smooth grass path from tee to green along which you are supposed to play "faultlessly") must be at least 30 yards (27 m) wide. This may not seem very wide, but most fairways are wider. A player who drives straight won't need more than 30-yards (27-m) width to stay on the fairway, and it's a good idea to aim to play in a 30-yard-wide (27-m) path (the "line of play") even if the fairway is 75 yards (68 m) wide. You'll save plenty of yardage by travelling straight.

I remember when my geometry teacher in high school showed me that a straight line is the shortest distance between two points. I got a lot out of geometry, and I still apply many of its principles to my golf game. It's obvious that if a golfer "laces the boot," as the pros call it, weaving back and forth across the fairway, he's losing yardage. He will also lose strokes to the player whose ball travels in straight (even though shorter) shots from tee to green.

PAR-4 HOLES

On a par-4 hole you are supposed to reach the green in 2 strokes. Let's say that your drive is straight down the middle and halfway there, as it should be. When you get to your ball, you find that it's in a little depression in the ground where the grass is soft and mushy. Do you take it out of that spot? No—you can't. The rules prohibit you from moving the ball. (We'll get to penalty strokes and "unplayable lies" later.) You must play it from that lie even if it means you can't possibly reach the green in one shot from there.

There are some players who move their ball from a bad lie, such as this, knowing full well it's against the rules. Don't do it! It's not only unfair to your opponent and yourself, but it will prevent you from learning how to play from a bad lie in a tournament. When you get to that stage, you *must* abide by the rules.

The only time you may move your ball from a bad lie on the fairway is when "winter rules" allow it. They go into effect during the late fall and winter, when branches are on the ground, when the regular greens are not being used, or when the ground is soft. Sometimes, when construction is going on, "ground-under-repair rules" will be placed temporarily on that hole or part of a hole. You are then allowed to move your ball from this marked area.

WHAT THE ROUGH IS FOR

As we said before, one way to keep your score down is to avoid trouble. However, golf courses are laid out so that you avoid trouble only by "faultless" play. If you hook or slice, you will go into the rough, and you'll be in trouble. Or if you don't drive the ball far enough from the tee you may land in the rough in front.

What exactly is the rough? Regulations require the rough along each fairway to consist only of fairly low grass for a 6-foot (2-m) width. Therefore, if your shot is only slightly off line you will get into the low rough, so called, and that is not too hard to get out of.

But beyond this 6-foot (2-m) strip of low rough (and in front of many tees for 100 yards or 90 m) comes the high or deep rough, which can be as wide and as rough as any uncultivated landscape. There may be bushes and stumps and rocks and swamp, trees and thorns and water. It's not easy to get out of deep rough, no matter how much you may like an adventure.

It's possible for a fairway to be lined with trees (even to have a tree or two in the middle), instead of allowing you 6 feet (2 m) of low rough. Even the most accurate golfer can't be sure of coming cleanly out of a maze of trees, so it's best to stay far away from the trees, no matter how shady and refreshing they appear to be.

Later on, we'll discuss the methods for getting your ball out of the rough. For the time being, let's just say that if you can find your ball at all in deep rough, you're lucky! You'll only lose one stroke getting out. A lost ball has to be counted as two strokes. You are supposed to return to the spot from which you hit the ball.

The accepted procedure for dropping a new ball after losing one in a hazard is to stand facing the green, at about the spot where your ball was lost and drop the new ball with a flip over your shoulder. You then play it from where it lies.

WATER HAZARDS

Did you ever try to hit anything from beneath the surface of water? Then you know that all you get is a splash. I've seen golfers who don't believe this. They find their ball in a creek, just beneath the surface of the water, so they wade in after it with a 9-iron and swipe at it. After a few futile tries, they stop trying to budge the ball, and pick it out, taking their penalty stroke.

Pros never try to play a ball out of water if it is 1 inch (25 mm) or more beneath the surface.

When you land in water or swamp or thick mud, take the ball out at once and take your penalty of 1 stroke good-naturedly. If you're in a pond or creek, you must place your ball (or a new one, if you can't find the first one) on the bank in back of the water, farther from the green. Even at that, you'll have a better chance to make up the stroke than by trying to blast it out of water.

If you hit your ball into the water from the tee, you must take a penalty stroke and tee up again, so that you are then playing your third stroke. Many beginners fail to count this extra stroke, and they come in with scores that sound good but really aren't. Whom are they fooling? Themselves. Until you can learn to play over water just as you play over ground, you aren't a golfer.

ARTIFICIAL HAZARDS—BUNKERS AND TRAPS

When a golf architect plans a course, he takes the available ground and shapes it up as best he can. On some holes, where he wants obstacles he finds only flat land. So here he creates hazards.

The hazard you'll become most familiar with is a sand trap (technically called a "bunker"). This can be anything from a depression 2 feet (60 cm) deep and lined with light sand, to a tremendous sand-filled pit whose lip is high above your head when you get down into it. The deeper the trap the harder it is to get out.

When you face the ball in a trap, you are not allowed to touch your club to the ground before you swing.

Some sand traps are strung like necklaces around the greens. This is to prevent you from rolling your ball onto the green with a dubbed (badly-hit) shot. The proper way to approach a green is to send the ball up into the air with a sharp arc and let it land on the green with backspin. If you are not accurate with this so-called "pitch" shot, you may land in a trap. If you don't have backspin on the ball, it may roll forward off the green and land in a trap. In either case, you're going to take an additional stroke getting on the green.

Another type of bunker is a mound or strip embankment, with or without a sand trap next to it. This type is usually placed off to the sides of a fairway (where you shouldn't be playing) or in the middle of a fairway at a spot which you should be clearing on the fly with your drive or second shot. Combined with natural hazards, such as hills, creeks, woods, bushes, and so on, these artificial hazards make a course interesting to play.

Architects plan hazards to make you play a *better* game, not to ruin your score. If you play the course perfectly, you won't land in a trap or behind a bunker the whole way around.

OUT-OF-BOUNDS AND WHAT IT MEANS

This term is applied to areas which are restricted to you, even if it is physically possible for you to enter them.

For example, a hole may be laid out with a hayfield adjoining the rough or fairway. Let's say a rock wall separates the course from the "out-of-bounds" hayfield which belongs to a farmer and is not a part of the course. If your ball lands there, you may not play it from there, but must shoot again from as near the original spot as possible, and count 2 strokes penalty.

If you think a shot has gone out-of-bounds, you may play a provisional ball (a "mulligan") at once from the same spot, but if the first was not out-of-bounds you must play that one.

If you go out-of-bounds while driving from the tee, you are required to hit another ball and count it as your third stroke. (Some courses may have local rules about this, so that you're only playing your second shot.) Straight hitters don't have to be concerned with out-of-bounds, generally.

Some courses are laid out with out-of-bounds markers placed in areas which would not normally be out-of-bounds. For instance, on a hole where there is plenty of wide-open fairway, out-of-bounds markers might be placed along one or both sides to keep you from slicing or hooking and not paying the penalty. This is one of the ways a course is made more difficult. There are other and better ways too.

INTRODUCING THE GREEN

We'll have a lot to say about greens in the section on putting. For the moment, let's just note that a green is an extremely important part of a course. An expert takes just about as many shots on the green as he does on all the other parts of the hole together. On an 18-hole course, you are allowed 36 putts out of, say, 72 par. So you should become well acquainted with greens!

The putting surface is smoother than any other of the grass surfaces on a course. The grass itself is of a different variety and it is kept close-cropped. Greenskeepers water the greens daily and continually. Sometimes, when you get to a green a hose will stretch across it and a sprinkler will be working. You may ask one of your playing partners to move this while you shoot, and then you move it while he and the others shoot, so it is out of the path of all players.

When a green is wet, it's slower to putt on than when it's dry and hard. The ball rolls more slowly because the moisture slows it down. As we'll see, it's easier to *pitch* to a wet green, and harder to *putt* on it.

The long putt on a rolling green is one of golf's hardest shots. You must figure out by knowledge and experience how a ball will roll on a sloping green, and then hit it accurately and powerfully enough for it to take a roller-coaster-like course into the cup or near it.

You will need plenty of study and experience with greens to become a perfect putter, even if you have great natural ability. You'll also have to learn to "read" greens—note their grain. But, right now, just remember that it's easier to get your ball into the cup when you're *on* the green than when you're on its edge, where the grass is not so close-cropped.

The pin itself stands in the cup. It should always be removed, by a fellow player or caddie, while you're putting. If you are far away and can't see the cup, let someone tip the pin in and then remove it as the ball nears it. The cup itself is $4\frac{1}{4}$ inches (106 mm) wide, about three times as wide as the ball (though at times you may not think so). You can't afford to be more than a hair off line with your putt, and still make the ball drop.

There's a good bit more to golf than knowing the course, but you're off to an excellent start.

3. Know Your Clubs

Not so many years ago a player bought one club at a time and accumulated his set by selecting clubs from different makers, most of whom were handcraftsmen. The shafts were of wood, and each had a different amount of "flex" to it.

Since the introduction of steel shafts and matched sets of clubs, the beginner can now select clubs of the same quality as the professional, and this has led to a vast improvement in scores of the average player. In a matched set you get the same amount of "flex" in each club, so you can swing exactly the same way and get the best results. Moreover, there is no chance of a steel shaft warping or causing a distortion in your stroke. Let's consider a few of the important items to check before you select your clubs.

THE "FLEX" OF A SHAFT

A golf club is made with a greater weight concentrated in the clubhead and sole than at any other point. The shaft enables you to transmit the power from the swing of your arms and body through your hands into the clubhead. This means that at some points of your swing the shaft is being pulled one way by your hands and the other way by the clubhead. The shaft therefore is like a stiff spring.

The amount of spring or resilience in the shaft is called its "flex," and there is always some flex in a shaft, even the stiffest steel shafts. Manufacturers make different kinds of shafts to give you more or less flex.

If you have a powerful and rapid swing with lots of wrist action, you give the shaft enough flex, without the shaft needing too much flex of its own. If you use a very flexible shaft with such a swing you will get too much variation in meeting the ball, and this leads to inaccuracy; so you need a stiff shaft.

On the other hand, if you have a slow and steady swing without much wrist action, you need a fairly flexible shaft.

How can you tell if a shaft is flexible or not? Snap the club-head in a short arc while holding the grip in the normal position, and bring it to an abrupt stop. If one club seems to swing farther after the abrupt stop than another, it has more flex.

Make sure the woods and irons you buy are matched as regards flex.

All fine shafts are easily recognized as having chrome finish and stepdowns. My preference is a shaft slightly firmer than average.

GETTING MEASURED FOR LENGTH

If a shaft is not the right length for you, it will never rest on the ground in the right position as you address the ball (prepare to swing at it). If the shaft is too short, you will bend over too far and your body will be all out of balance. If the shaft is too long, you will swing with too long an arc and you will lose accuracy.

To get the right-length shaft, test a driver this way: Let it rest with its sole absolutely flat on the ground or any level surface. Stretch out and place your hands on the grip in the position you will take to swing the club. If you are standing up straight now, and your hands are as high as your waist, the shaft is too long for you. If you are bent over more than a trifle, the shaft is too short for you. If you are balanced and comfortable with your hands out and your back just slightly bent, then the shaft is about the right length.

To make perfectly sure the shaft is right, let a professional fit you the way a tailor does. Or let a friend watch you as you measure yourself for your clubs.

After you get the right-length driver, you will find that the rest of the matched set will fit you too.

JUDGING WEIGHT

I usually suggest that a beginner choose clubs which are a little too light for him. The reason? Because a light club is easier to swing than a heavy one. You can get more wrist action and body power into your swing with a light club.

However, a club that is too light—for instance, a woman's club for a boy of 145 lbs. (65 kilos)—will make you fall into error, and you will press too hard to get distance.

A club that is too heavy is dragged somewhat because your muscles can't handle it easily. If you try to overcome this by speeding up your swing, you will hit the ball too soon in the arc of your swing. (More on this later.)

Therefore, in choosing your first set of clubs, get those that are light enough for you to swing easily. One word of caution here: if you are not buying a set, but have received an older set for a gift, be sure it's the right weight for you before taking it out on the course. Have it cut down in a pro shop if it isn't right.

GETTING THE RIGHT GRIP

Most clubs are made with leather or composition grips. (Some have finger grooves in the grip all ready for the person whose hand fits. Don't get ready-made grips as they are illegal for U.S.G.A. tournaments.) If you're still growing, your hands are growing too and it's better to get leather grips, which you can change by yourself as you grow. You can keep adding gauzetex under the leather wrapping. Most grips are larger at the top of the shaft, so they are easier to grasp with your left hand. Consider the fact that your hands must overlap on the grip, and be sure you get a grip that's tapered enough for you to get a comfortable, solid grasp of the club.

The spongy type of grip doesn't help too much in preventing jarring. If you hit the ball accurately, you won't feel any jar at all in your hands. If you hit it wrong, no grip is going to prevent jarring. Therefore, choose a firm leather rather than a spongy one.

SELECTING THE WOODS

Drivers made today usually have a deep face. Older drivers were shallow—that is, the faces had depth only about the equivalent of our 3-wood today, though the angle of loft was the same 8 to 11 degrees.

The deep face allows you to tee your ball higher and thus get more loft that way. Don't choose a shallow face, as you'll have to tee lower. You will gain confidence by having a deep-faced driver. (If you prefer, begin by using a 3-wood from the tee, and you'll surely get loft.)

The No. 3-wood or "spoon" got its nickname from the degree of the loft. On the fairway, it has to zip through the grass, taking a small strip divot (piece of sod from the top layer of the ground in front of the ball) after you hit the ball. Because of this, the 3-wood is made with a shallower face than a driver, and with greater loft. Again, be sure you choose a club with enough depth when you select your set of woods.

The woods should be matched, and therefore your No. 4-wood will be similar to the 3-wood but with still more loft. If you get a No. 5-wood in your set, it will probably have a smaller head than the 4-wood. It takes the place of a 2-iron and is used where you need distance and still have to get the ball up in the air quickly.

The shaft of the driver is longer than any other club in your bag—43 inches (109.2 cm) is the standard length. The other woods decrease by $\frac{1}{2}$ inches (13 mm), 3-wood 42$\frac{1}{2}$ (108 cm), 4-wood 42 (106.7 cm), and 5-wood 41$\frac{1}{2}$ (105.4 cm).

MATCHING THE IRONS

Sometimes you can get a set of iron clubs (they're really made of steel) that matches the woods, and then you will have no worry about flex, length, etc.

Later on we will discuss the various irons in greater detail, but for the time being, let's say that you don't need a full set to start with. You'll want a 3-iron, 5-iron, 7-iron, 9-iron or a pitching wedge, and a putter. If you can find a matched set that you can add to later, fine!

Here again, be sure you get clubs that are light enough for you to swing easily. If there is too much head weight (at the bottom), you may find them comfortable at the start and then wearying later.

Select your iron set by swinging a heavy iron, the 9-iron or 7-iron. If these are comfortable for you, then try out the others. If you choose on the basis of the lighter 3-iron you may go wrong on the short irons, but it isn't as likely to happen the other way around. The 2-iron is lightest and as the numbers increase so do the weight and loft.

MARKINGS

The designs which manufacturers place on clubfaces are put there for a purpose, particularly on irons. Choose clubs with mesh, dot or stripe markings in a close and regular pattern, and stay away from extra-fancy markings. The idea is to prevent the ball from sliding off the clubface when it is hit, and you only need to be sure there are markings wherever you may hit the ball on the clubface.

The insets on woods need not be fancy either, but the markings should be deeply enough cut into the inset so you get the benefit from them. Some insets are made of composition material. Try to choose woods with insets, as they preserve the faces of your clubs. The faces of cheaper clubs without insets sometimes wear down just after you've become accustomed to them.

TOOLS OF THE TRADE

Have you ever thought that your spiked shoes are just as important as your clubs? If you can't anchor your feet to get a good stance, if your shoes are too loose and you "swim around" in them, or if they're too tight and pinch you from the 12th hole on, or if they're so heavy that you tire easily, you'll never play a good game. A good foundation for your feet is essential as golf is a walking game. Invest in one good pair of spiked shoes.

Similarly, if you persist in wearing the latest shirt fashion and it turns out to be tight under your arms, you won't be able to swing properly. I don't object to fine clothes, but first of all they must be comfortable and allow you freedom to swing a golf club.

To be comfortable, a girl should choose shorts or slacks or a comfortably full skirt. The blouse or dress top should have an action-free (full) back.

If the sun is strong, you'll need a hat or cap, but preferably one that won't get in your way or be too heavy on your head.

4. Your Swing

You can learn a lot of golf from a book, but one important thing you can learn better from a teacher is the swing. If you have an opportunity to take a few lessons from a professional golf teacher, by all means do it. Take these lessons on the swing before you go out on the course to play. The beginner who learns the swing without a book and without a pro to teach him can learn only by trial and error—mostly error—and will get into incorrect habits that are difficult to straighten out later on.

Almost all pros play alike and think alike on major points, such as the swing, and this book will parallel what the pro teaches you. If you can't obtain a personal instructor, then study this chapter carefully. Have a friend watch your swing, or better yet, have him or her learn golf with you! You can take turns as pupil and teacher, following the book to see if you're learning correctly.

TIMING—DON'T HURRY!

The first thing to remember is that the golf ball is sitting still and you're in no hurry to hit it. It isn't like a baseball, coming at you full speed from the pitcher's mound. It will stay right where it is until you stroke it away with your club. Because you're in no hurry, you can make your swing a thing of beauty and grace—as rhythmic as if you were swinging to music, and as smooth as a fresh breeze.

The next important point to remember is that your swing is always the same. It consists of five parts (address, backswing, downswing, impact, and follow-through, in that order) and these parts may be different in length and force, but the swing is essentially the same all the time, with a wood club or an iron. You start swinging back slowly, hesitate at the top point, then swing down with increasing speed through the point of impact, after which you follow through with decreasing power. It's always the same.

HOW TO KNOW WHERE YOU ARE SHOOTING

You start by addressing the ball—that is, you place your clubhead so that its sole is flat on the ground, centered directly in back of the ball. What do we mean "in back" of the ball?

Let's imagine that a line has been drawn from the spot where your ball is resting to the hole you're shooting for. This would be called "the line of flight" and you want to address the ball by putting your club on an extension of that line, in back of the ball. Your swing will follow that line of flight to some extent, because you want to hit the ball straight.

Your addressing of the ball must be perfectly straight, or you will hit the ball at an angle to the correct line of flight. A slight difference in angle at this point will widen considerably 100 yards (90 m) out, as you know if you paid attention to your geometry lessons.

HOW TO STAND

Your feet at address should be almost perpendicular to the line of flight and your hips should be parallel to it. We'll get to variations in the stance for each particular shot as we take up the various clubs, but for the time being let's assume you're using a driver or 3-wood. Your feet will be placed in a natural spread, about as wide apart as your shoulders, and the toes of your shoes (pointed slightly outwards, as in a duck walk) will be up to a line parallel to the line of flight for the ball. This is called the square (or closed) stance.

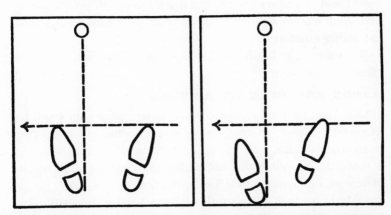

(Left) In the square stance, your toes should point slightly outward but square with the line of flight. (Right) In the open stance, used for short iron shots, the ball should still be lined up with your left heel, and the stance is no wider, in fact not as wide. Your stance is "opened" by drawing your forward foot back from the line of flight.

At address, your weight should be on your heels, equally on each. Your knees should be loose and in a slight squat. Avoid tenseness at all times, but especially in your stance. Your feet should be placed comfortably on level ground (if possible) and the spikes of your shoes should be settled into the turf once you take the right position.

What is the right distance to stand from the ball? This is easy to figure out, though many beginners think it's difficult. With your clubhead flat on its sole, centered in the proper position behind the ball, grasp the shaft near its end with the fingers of your left hand. Now step with your left foot into a position where your left elbow is resting against your left hip as you stand straight up, still grasping the shaft. That is the right distance for you. If you now grasp the shaft with your right hand just below your left, it will force you to bend slightly, and your elbows will come away from your hips so that you can swing comfortably.

(Of course, a left-handed player uses his right hand to "line up" his stance.)

HANDS AND HEAD AT ADDRESS

Once you have taken the correct stance, your hands will be in correct relation to your body—6 to 8 inches (15 to 20 cm) from your belt line—far enough away from your hips to allow a comfortable swing and not so far that you have to reach. Where should your hands be in relation to the ball? Just a fraction of an inch (a few millimetres) ahead of the ball. This means that the shaft of your club, when you're in the address position, will not be absolutely perpendicular to the line of flight, but will be at a slight angle. (The hand position for a drive, as we will see later, is slightly different, with your club-head farther forward and your hands just behind the ball.)

Don't forget that your head is part of your body—not only for brain power, but also as a pivotal point in your swing. Your head will move less than any other part of your body, and so you must get it set in the right position with your left eye directly above the ball and your chin turned just a fraction of an inch (a few millimetres) away from the hole. You've heard the golf saying, "Keep your head down!" The way to keep it down is to put it down at address and concentrate on the ball, continuing to watch the spot where it was even after you hit it away! Your caddie or someone else can follow its flight for you.

HOW TO GRIP THE CLUB

All right now. You're lined up with your clubhead behind the ball, your feet set, your weight back, your head down, your arms out, and your body and shoulders in a slight crouch. You're ready to take your grip on the club and swing it.

Up to this point, you've been grasping the shaft lightly. Now you must take a solid grip on the shaft, because you want to make the club act as if it were a part of your body, carrying the force and power of your hands, arms and body motion into a strong smash. If your grip is slippery or too relaxed, a good part of the power will not be transmitted to the ball, and the club may twist or even fly out of your hands.

Undoubtedly you have swung a bat. Most boys and girls have a chance some time in childhood to play baseball or cricket or softball and learn the batter's swing. If you're right-handed, you place your left hand near the end of your bat and your right hand along the shaft a little farther. In baseball, your hands don't overlap at all. There are some golfers who grip the club exactly that way, but most modern-day golfers use an overlapping grip. (A few use an interlocking grip, which I recommend for players with small hands.)

As you place the clubhead in address position with your left hand, the knuckle side of your left hand should be facing the hole and the shaft should cross your hand diagonally. The fingers of your left hand should then be wrapped around the underneath part of the shaft, with your left thumb slightly to the right of the top of the shaft. This is a palm and finger grip, with the pressure points on the last three fingers. (See diagram on next page.)

Now, place your right hand on the shaft as if you were shaking hands with the club. Start by wrapping your pinky beneath the knuckle of your left forefinger. Grasp the shaft with the other fingers of your right hand, making sure they are beneath the shaft, except that your right thumb should be slightly to the left of the top of the shaft. Pressure points of this hand are the thumb and forefinger. As you look down, see if the V-shape angle between your right thumb and forefinger points to your right shoulder. If so, your hands are in the correct position.

To complete your grip, increase the pressure of your fingers on the shaft. This will make your grip firm and solid to hit with. Wiggle your wrists a little and make certain that the club is firm in your grip. Now you can relax your arm muscles,

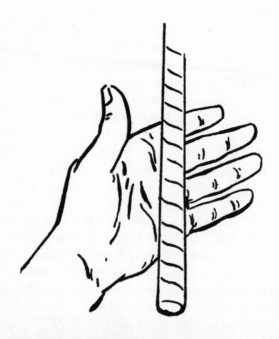

When grasping the club with your left hand, let the shaft cross your palm diagonally. A proper grip is with your fingers and palm, not just with your fingers alone.

but keep the club firm in your fingers without squeezing. The clubhead is going to do the work for you, and you are going to hold firmly onto the shaft as the club performs.

The diagram below shows you exactly how the fingers overlap, with the little finger of your right hand on top of the

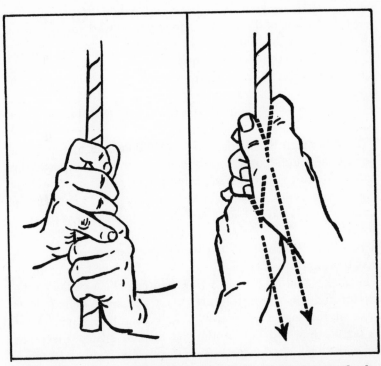

(Left) How the overlapping grip looks from beneath the shaft. Your little finger should overlap the knuckle of the forefinger of your other hand. (Right) Seen from the top of the shaft, the grip should form a V between the thumb and forefinger of each hand, and these V's should point to your right shoulder. You will always place your thumb in the right position if you watch the V's.

forefinger of your left hand. This tends to unify your hands and give you a firm grasp of the club. A golf shaft is thinner than the hand of a bat and you can overlap easily.

THE BACKSWING

You start your swing back not by moving the clubhead first, but by a "forward press." This is somewhat of a relaxing action made by moving your right knee and hands forward a trifle towards the line of flight. This allows you to start the clubhead off the ground, back into the first phase of its arc.

Since your hands were slightly in front of the ball to start with, at the end of the forward press they are still farther in front. Now, with your left forearm doing the work (or at least feeling as if it were doing all the work) you pull the clubhead back low and close to the ground.

You don't go back exactly straight along the line of flight because, if you did, only your hands and arms would power the ball. You must get your body into the swing, by pivoting your hips as you swing. Your right hip goes back and your left hip forward as you pivot back, but remember to keep your head down!

In order to accomplish the backswing properly you have to take the clubhead back slightly *inside* your intended line of flight. This makes the arc of your swing a tilted orbit parallel to the line of flight in the hitting area, and well back behind your head at the top of your swing, after your hips have turned as far as they will go. At the top of your swing (the point beyond which your arms will not go comfortably with your left arm straightened out), your wrists will cock automatically, but will not turn!

THE TOP OF YOUR SWING

Let's stop a moment and examine this "topswing point." Your left shoulder should be directly under your chin. Your chest should be facing almost squarely back, away from the hole. Your left arm should be practically straight at the elbow. Your right arm should be well bent at the elbow and only a few inches (centimetres) away from your hip. Your weight should be on the heel and outside of your right foot, and your right knee should be somewhat stiffened. Your left knee should be bent and pointing at the ball, and your left heel will then be up off the ground with only the ball of your left foot on the ground. Your wrists will be cocked, and the club firmly in your grip.

(Left) In the backswing, you should feel your left forearm doing the work. (Right) After reaching the topswing point, you start the downswing by bringing your weight down on your left heel. It looks like you're "sitting down to the ball."

Don't worry about where the topswing point will be. The length of your club shaft will determine that when you take a full swing. The driver has the longest shaft and so the arc of its swing will be the widest and the topswing point will be farther back than with any other club.

There are situations which we will discuss fully later on when you take a *shortened* swing with a long club. For instance, if you think you can reach the green with a short 7-iron shot, you can decide to come back only halfway (up to hip level) with the clubhead and cock your wrists at that point. With less swing, you get less power.

THE DOWNSWING

There is a moment of hesitation at the top of your swing. You start the downswing with the same feeling of your left forearm and shoulder doing the work. Good players seem to "sit down" to the ball at this point.

To get your downswing started right, it's a good idea to shift your weight consciously at the top of your swing from your right foot to your left by bringing your left heel down to the ground with a snap. This straightens your left knee out, and gives you a "solid left side" to hit with. This means that your left arm remains straightened at the elbow throughout the whole downswing.

What is happening to your hips? As your arms sweep down, your hips are pivoting back rhythmically into the position they held at address. In this pivot, they are moving rapidly and giving you body power with which to lash at the ball. Many beginners are afraid to pivot their hips enough and so they don't get enough "steam" behind their shots. Arms and wrists alone can't do all the work.

How about your wrists? They must stay cocked until your clubhead actually enters the hitting area (12 inches or 30 cm from the ball), and then they snap forward with tremendous power as the clubhead makes impact with the ball.

Your body at impact is in the position of address, except that your weight is on your left side.

POINT OF IMPACT

Suppose you are planning to hit a nail on the head with a hammer. You draw the hammer back and then swing it forward. If you hold back at the point of contact and use just enough power to bop the nail on its head, it won't go very far into the wood. But if you figure on hitting the nailhead with more power than is needed just to reach it (that is, if you hit "through" the nailhead) with the hammer, you'll drive the nail far into the wood. The weight and force of the hammer striking the nail is what drives it in. Just hitting it on the head won't drive it.

It's the same way with a golf club and golf ball. If you figure on bringing your club around and just reaching the ball with it, you'll tap the ball all right but it won't fly far. If, on the other hand, you figure on hitting "through" the ball with every bit of your power, you'll drive it out into the air with plenty of speed and zip.

The power of your shot is determined by the force and speed with which your clubhead hits the ball at one point only—the point of impact. If you have a balanced swing, and bring the clubhead into the hitting area correctly, you will make the right impact with the ball. You cannot afford to relax your grip at the point of impact, no matter how perfect your swing. You must aim for that moment, that fleeting second at which your clubhead drives into the ball. It's too fast for the human eye to see, but keep looking as if you *could* see it.

You must always hit the back of the ball. Just stop and figure this out. You want the ball to go forward—therefore you hit it from the back, square in the back. If you hit it on top, it will tend to go down into the ground, even though it may also move forward. If you hit it on the side of the back, it will go off to one side. You must hit it squarely in the back at the point of impact.

HOW TO FOLLOW THROUGH

The easiest thing in golf is the "follow-through." If you hit "through" the ball, you can't help but follow through correctly. If you stop or half-stop your swing at the point of impact, you won't get a full swing and your follow-through will be shortened. Your head will come up too soon, and this means that your stroke has not been perfectly made.

The follow-through is the *result* of your swing, and though we usually consider it part of the swing it really cannot affect the flight of your ball. The ball has already been hit. If it's been hit correctly, you'll follow through correctly. If not, your follow-through won't correct it.

One little hint may help you here: Make believe that you're hitting two golf balls, one an inch (25 mm) or so in front of the other. The back one is your real ball. You hit that first, and as your clubhead sweeps through it must also hit the other ball directly in front of it. If you imagine you're doing this

(Opposite, top left) This is the cocked position of your wrists at the midpoint of your downswing, as seen in the dotted line in the drawing at the top right. (Top right) Your wrists should be kept cocked until the clubhead enters the hitting area, 12 inches (30 cm) from the ball, as seen in the solid line drawing. Then they should be snapped quickly to meet the back of the ball at point of impact (see lower left), giving the shot maximum power from your body, arms and wrists. (Lower right) A full follow-through is automatic as you "hit through the ball."

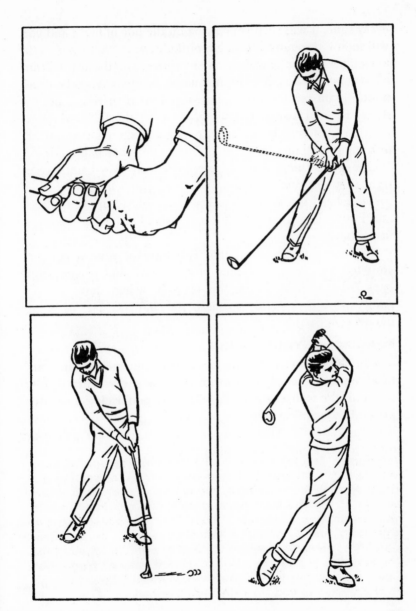

every time, it will keep your swing on the line of flight and you will follow through on the line of flight, too.

Don't let up after the point of impact. Let the momentum of your swing carry you through as far as it will. Then hold the position you reach on the follow-through. If there has been a defect in your swing, it will show up in the follow-through position—you may be too much on your toes, too far bent over, or some such thing. Hold the position until your ball lands.

One more thing. Your head should stay down until your right shoulder comes around and forces your chin up. Picking up your head too soon will pull your clubhead up off the arc, and it will skim the top of the ball instead of hitting it square in the back.

You end the follow-through with most of your weight on your left foot. You have now made an arc that is complete: back from address to the top of your swing, down to the point of impact, and through the ball as far as your momentum carries you.

PRACTICING YOUR SWING

You can't watch your own swing without picking up your head, even if you use a mirror, and it's not wise to try it. Let someone else watch you and see if you're performing correctly, preferably someone who knows the swing and doesn't just *think* he knows it. Make sure he reads this chapter and gets the swing right in his own mind first.

5. Length with Your Woods

You might think it logical to start by learning how to hit with your driver. But the drive is something special in golf. It's the only shot you always make from a tee (wooden peg on which the ball is set above the ground) and there is no other shot quite like it. A driver is one club which has little loft in the angle of its face.

I find that beginners who first learn driving from a tee have trouble mastering the fairway and other shots later, but the reverse procedure of learning always is successful.

Therefore, let's assume that you have made a beautiful 200-yard (180-m) drive from the tee, and your ball has landed on the fairway on short but firm grass, still 200 yards (180 m) from the green. You walk up to the ball and see that it is lying on flat ground (not in a depression) and you choose to hit with your 3-wood and see if you can land the ball on the green.

HOW TO USE THE 3-WOOD

You take your stance with the ball lined up inside the heel of your left foot when you are playing a 3-wood shot.

Follow the directions for the swing given in the last chapter. Address the ball, go through the backswing, downswing, hit the ball and follow through. In this particular shot, you want to catch the ball squarely in the back (as on all shots) but more exactly you want to catch the ball just a little bit before the club reaches the very bottom of the downswing. In other words, you want to hit down on the ball with your 3-wood.

Why? By hitting down, you will send the ball up! Yes, the angle of the 3-wood face does the trick. Actually, although the club is travelling down at this point, it also is travelling forward at great speed. When you hit the back of the ball a blow with the angled clubface, you will send the ball spinning up into the air, with a backspin motion. (We'll go more thoroughly into the backspin in the chapter on iron play.)

The very bottom of the arc of your swing will hit a point a fraction of an inch (a few millimetres) below the turf, at the exact spot where the ball had been resting. The metal plate on the sole of this club helps you to cut through the turf. You will not lose any power by hitting the ground, because you have already hit the ball by the time you touch the ground! When you hit the ball properly, you will take a divot (strip of turf torn loose) *after* the ball has been hit. If you take a divot before you hit the ball, it certainly will deflect the club from its arc and cause loss of power.

The proper divot for a 3-wood shot is about $\frac{1}{4}$ inch (6 mm) wide and perhaps 2 inches (50 mm) long, and not more than $\frac{1}{4}$ inch (6 mm) deep. If you have lined up your stance correctly, you'll hit the ball right and take the right divot. It isn't as complicated as it may sound.

You hit down on the ball with all your wood shots (except the drive) and with all your irons because you will get more accuracy that way.

If you try to sweep the ball off the fairway with a 3-wood (catching it at the bottom of the arc), you may achieve the desired result a great percentage of the time. But if there is an impediment in the way, seen or unseen, you will perhaps not get the ball up into the air. Also, if you sweep it off, you will get a forward spin and forward roll when the ball hits. If it should land on the green, it would roll right off again. With backspin, the ball will stick to the green in all likelihood.

HOW TO USE THE 4-WOOD AND 5-WOOD

You take the same swing with these woods as with the 3-wood, and you hit down on the ball for the same reasons, taking just a little more divot perhaps with these clubs.

When would you use a 4-wood in preference to a 3-wood? When the distance to the green is shorter, or when you need more loft to get over an obstacle. Also, you might use a 4-wood when the ball is in a shallow hole, though a 3-iron or 5-iron would be safer in such a spot. If the grass is soft and high, you might prefer a 4-wood to a 3-wood, but a 5-wood might be safer, as the clubhead is smaller.

Beginners should not use woods in the rough, but as you get

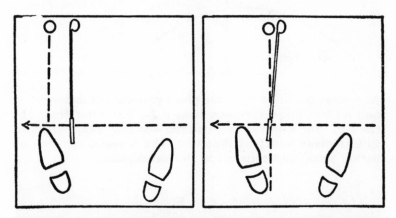

(Left) For a drive off a tee, get your ball in line with the toe of your left shoe, and keep your hands a little in back of the ball. (Right) With all the other woods, get your ball in line with your left heel, and put your hands slightly in front of the ball.

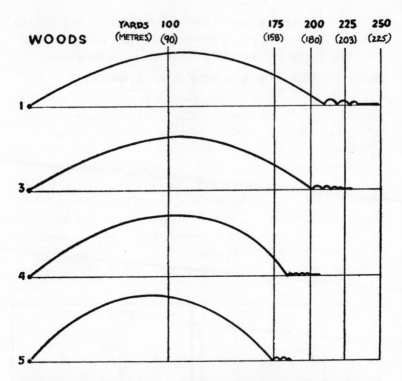

WOODS	YARDS (METRES)	100 (90)		175 (158)	200 (180)	225 (203)	250 (225)

Note that the drive off a tee gives you about the same loft and a little more distance than a 3-wood shot from the fairway. For a higher arc, use the 4-wood; even when hit full, it gives you less distance. The 5-wood reaches an earlier peak, and thus gives shorter distance.

more experience you may want to use the 4-wood when you land in rough that has sparse grass, but is a good distance from the green. A 4-wood gives you less distance than a 3-wood, but more than a long iron. The club will swish through the rough all right, and the ball will fly out if you can take a divot with your wood club. If the ground is hard, it's better to make sure of taking a divot, and use an iron with medium loft, such as a 5-iron.

In taking your stance for a 4-wood shot, get the ball in the same position as for a 3-wood. However, you will have to stand closer to the ball than with a 3-wood, because the shaft is $\frac{1}{2}$ inch (13 mm) shorter, you will remember.

For a 5-wood, you stand still closer because of the still shorter shaft, but play this shot in the same position as for all fairway wood shots.

Getting the ball up into the air is the important thing with a wood shot. It will travel much greater distances than it possibly can by rolling along the ground and losing momentum every time it bounces.

You may find that you get more accuracy with irons than with woods. In this case, use irons when you have an even choice. The shorter the shaft the more accuracy you'll get, in general. However, if you can use your woods from the fairway with a fair degree of accuracy, you'll get distance without pressure.

THE ALL-IMPORTANT DRIVE

Now we are ready to concentrate on the drive, the tee shot. First of all, practice with your 3-wood from the tee so you get into the habit of obtaining loft. Then when you are letter-perfect with the 3-wood, shift to the driver, with its deeper face and less loft. Getting the ball up in the air, in a sweeping rainbow-like arc, is going to be your main problem from the tee. Some players never switch from the 3-wood to the driver, and use the 3-wood regularly on tee or fairway. You may want to do that, especially during your first few rounds of play.

When you tee up the ball, make sure the tee is securely in the ground and its top is about even with the top of the club. This will allow your clubhead to get sufficiently beneath the ball to impart overspin to it. Also the ball won't be teed so high that you sweep entirely beneath it. You want it teed so you hit the back of the ball squarely with the center of the inset of your club, and you need make no effort to get the ball up in the air. You want to let the clubhead and clubface do the work for you. Practice teeing at different heights to see which is best for *you*.

In other words, although you are going to sweep the ball off the tee, instead of hitting down on it, you don't want to have to lift the clubhead up. You can't possibly lift the ball up with the club—you can only hit it with a sweeping motion. This means that you will make contact with the ball at the bottommost point of your downswing, and you will not touch the ground. Overspin will then keep your ball rolling towards the green after it hits the ground.

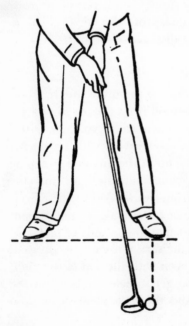

The drive is the only shot with a wood that is a sweep. You want to get overspin, and thus more roll with your drive. The way to do it is to keep your standard swing but play the ball off your left toe and hit slightly on your upswing.

Of course, the length of your drive depends to a certain extent on your ball. I personally prefer a premium ball such as a Titleist, Hogan or Ram.

Let's drive a ball. With a 3-wood or driver, address the ball. It should be in line with your left toe. You take your square stance and overlapping grip. Then swing as outlined in the last chapter. At the point of impact, you should have your hands back in address position, your wrists snapping and your body pivot unleashed, with all the power of your arms, hands and body concentrated on hitting the back of the ball squarely. Your left eye is on the tiny spot on back of the ball, and you are imagining a second ball in front of the real one which you must also sweep off the tee.

It's as easy as that. Once the rudiments of your swing become natural to you, you'll be able to drive and play wood shots from the fairway with equal skill. The drive is the only shot in golf (except for the putt and the chip shot with an iron) that is more a sweep than a down-hit.

HOW TO CORRECT FAULTS

Topping

The most common error in a young player's game is a tendency to top the ball. Usually this occurs from picking up your head too soon, and you know how to prevent that—hold your head down until your right shoulder comes around and pushes your chin up.

Another cause of topping is an involuntary pulling back of your hands at the point of impact. If you imagine the second ball in front of the real one, and hit both, you won't pull back or half-stop. Still another reason for topping is failure to snap your wrists when the clubhead enters the hitting area. This causes you to hit the ball with the face half turned away, and only the bottom edge of the face will touch the ball. If you flick your wrists in time, you'll bring the face firmly into the ball and not into the top of the ball. Of course, if you look at the top of the ball instead of the back, you'll tend to hit the top, and you don't want to do that.

A topped ball either rolls only a comparatively few yards (metres), or hops up into the air and then comes down quickly. However, topping is easy to overcome if you follow the above comments carefully.

Slicing

Many players tend to "slice" their drives and wood shots— that is, hit them with glancing blows so they spin off to the right of the line of flight. This is the result of hitting the ball with too-open a clubface at the point of impact. It can be caused by a number of things.

You may not be snapping your wrists from their cocked position the moment you enter the hitting area, and instead of topping you're slicing. Your hands may be too far ahead of the ball, or too far ahead of your body in its swing and pivot, thus bringing the clubhead into the ball before your power is concentrated there. For another thing you may not be facing the ball with a square stance. Your left foot may be back from the line of flight or pointed too much towards the green. In any case, you can usually correct a slice by moving your right foot back from the line of flight—this doesn't correct the other things you're doing wrong, but just counteracts the slice.

There are more reasons for slicing, some of them uncorrectable by changing your stance. For instance, if your left elbow is not straight at point of impact, the clubface will point off to the right. Also, if you are "pushing" too much on the downswing with your right hand and arm, instead of letting your left forearm do the work, you'll push the clubface across the ball and slice it off with a backspin. One correctable fault is placing your right hand too far to the left of the shaft—in which case the V would point to your chin and not to your right shoulder.

Let an expert or a friend watch you hit a few balls if you're slicing, and he will soon see what it is you're doing wrong.

Hooking

You may be hitting with a "hook," which is the opposite of a slice. The ball may be curving off to the left of the line of flight. This is the result of hitting the ball with a "closed" face. If you hook consistently, you can correct it somewhat by opening your stance—pulling your left foot back from the line of flight.

The cause of your hook may lie in "rolling" too much with your right arm, and not letting your left arm guide the club squarely into the ball. Your body pivot may be ahead of your hands. Your wrists may be rolled, instead of cocked and un-cocked. A correctable fault is placing your right hand too far under the shaft—in which case the V would point to your right hip, instead of to your right shoulder.

Let someone note the position of the clubface at the top of your swing—if it's not at a 45-degree angle to the line of flight, you'll either hook or slice.

To get a straight-flying shot you'll have to overcome fatigue, so don't handicap yourself additionally with bad habits, such as those outlined above. Don't even think about doing things wrong. In fact, forget this section until you find you have a fault that needs correcting. You'll know this section is here, and you can refer to it.

SHOULD YOU GO FOR POWER?

There is some disagreement among the pros over whether a beginner should try for power and distance in his wood shots right from the beginning. I'm inclined to the view that you'll get distance more readily if you make the proper contact with the ball. If you let the clubhead do the work, and don't press or squeeze, the ball will zoom off and climb into a graceful arc as only a well-hit wood shot can. If a beginner doesn't use the power of his pivot and wrist snap, of course he's not hitting the ball with the maximum power. But to strive for power, to a beginner, it usually means putting on pressure, and that is not the way to learn how to use your woods.

I know a number of elderly gentlemen who have little strength left in their wrists, and can hardly turn their hips, but they power the ball 200 yards (180 m) straight down the fairway on occasion, and consistently hit 180 yards (162 m), just because they know how to meet the ball. Timing the hit is the way to get power.

Get accuracy and timing and let the length take care of itself!

6. Accuracy with Your Irons

Many golfers get such a thrill out of hitting a long ball that they think that's all there is to the game. Don't be misled by duffers who try to sock the ball 200 yards (180 m) regularly no matter what club they're using. Just watch where they land—mostly in the rough! It may be fun to take a 5-iron (mashie) which is supposed to give you 155 yards (140 m), and power the ball 180 yards (162 m) with it, but it's not golf.

Each of the ten irons (you'll probably carry only four or five at the start) is made to hit the ball a certain distance, and make it travel with a certain arc.

Study the chart on page 62 and note that each club gives you 10 yards (9 m) more or less than the next in rank. Then study each club, the length of its shaft, the angle of its face, its weight, its markings. Then swing it until you get the feel of it. Go through all the irons in your bag and swing them in practice before you hit a ball with them.

You are after accuracy with your irons. That means you must become so well acquainted with each club that it's like a friend to you. Each time you hit the ball with an iron you must know how far it will go and where it will land. The only way to find out is to get experience with each club. Always hit the ball with the same swing and the same pressure. If you "press" one time and hit the ball 10 yards (9 m) farther, you may press too hard the next time and slice it off the fairway. You want to find out how far *you* generally hit a 3-iron, for example, and you're not interested in how far your friends hit theirs. So you go out to a practice range, hit a number of shots with your 3-iron and you find that, without pressing, the shots go from, say, 170 to 180 yards (153 to 162 m), or 175 yards (158 m) average. That's the range of the club for you.

I always remember how Babe Didrikson Zaharias learned this lesson. While breaking in, her desire was to be an extra-long hitter. She would close up the face of any iron, toe it in and half top the ball 10 or 20 yards (9 or 18 m) farther than she should have. When she stopped trying to set distance records, she brought her score down. She realized that previously she had only been kidding herself. When her "pressing" days were over, she went on to develop a fine grooved swing and a splendid golf game.

Nobody ever hears of distance records set with irons. Nor will anyone be impressed by one tremendous sock you get with the wrong club. During your first five years of golf, always rely on getting there with a *longer* club than may be necessary.

THE IRON CLUBS IN YOUR BAG

If you are about to buy a set of clubs, choose four irons besides your putter—a 3-iron, a 5-iron, a 7-iron and either a 9-iron or pitching wedge. These are the clubs you'll find the most use for.

The 3-iron is used mostly for long shots from the fairway. The 5-iron is used for long, high shots to the green, and for coming out of the rough. The 7-iron is for pitch shots and chip shots to the green, and the 9-iron (or wedge) is to pitch and get out of sand traps or very heavy rough.

As your game improves, you will want to add the other

medium-length irons—the 4-iron and 6-iron—to give you greater range with the long approach shots. Later on, you may want both 9-iron and pitching wedge, as well as a sand wedge and probably a 2-iron for greater length on long fairway shots. You probably won't want a 1-iron (driving iron) as this is the most difficult club to handle in the entire bag; it has little loft and is used mostly in wind by professionals. You will seldom have a situation where you need a 1-iron instead of a 3-wood or a driver.

The 3-iron will give you more loft than the conventional 2-iron.

EXAMINE YOUR IRONS

Take a look at your set of irons. The first thing you notice is that the higher the number the greater the slant of the club's face. The 5-iron is sloped at a much greater angle than the 3-iron. The 7-iron is much more "open" than the 5-iron, and the 9-iron practically lies down when you let the club rest on its sole.

Why is this? For one reason only—to give the ball loft when you hit it. The more the loft the greater the backspin. Don't worry too much about backspin, because it is automatically taken care of, if you hit the ball properly.

Of course, the higher the ball goes up, the less ground distance it can cover. So the high-loft clubs (7, 8 and 9) give you short distance and lots of backspin. The medium-loft clubs (4, 5 and 6) give you greater distance and less backspin. The long irons (1, 2 and 3) give you about the same loft as the same-number wood clubs, and impart backspin if the ball is hit properly.

Now look at your irons again. Note the markings on the face. Yours may be horizontal stripes or dots or a mesh pattern or something fancier. These not only make the clubs look smart, but they're manufactured this way for a purpose—to give greater backspin to the ball. (Keep the markings clean.) The ball itself has similar markings for exactly the same reasons. If the clubface were smooth and the ball as plain as a table-tennis ball, there would be no certainty of accuracy in a well-executed stroke. The ball might slide across the clubface, and go off at a tangent or with an overspin. The earliest golf clubs were made smooth-faced, but recent improvements in design have made it easier to play iron shots accurately.

Look once again at your irons. Note that the longer-range clubs have longer shafts. The shaft of your 3-iron is a good deal longer than that of your 9-iron. This is because you will take a longer swing to get greater distance.

Also note that the weight of the short-range clubs is concentrated more at the sole, and the long-range irons have the weight across the back. This is also to help you get the proper swing and loft.

DISTANCE TABLE

Here's a table to help you get an idea of the length your iron clubs will give you.

	Regular		Maximum		Minimum	
	yards	metres	yards	metres	yards	metres
1-iron	195	176	220	198	—	—
2-iron	185	167	195	176	155	140
3-iron	175	158	185	167	140	126
4-iron	165	149	175	158	125	113
5-iron	155	140	165	149	110	99
6-iron	145	131	155	140	90	81
7-iron	130	117	145	131	80	72
8-iron	120	108	135	122	70	63
9-iron	110	99	120	108	50	45
Pitching wedge	100	90	100	90	?	?

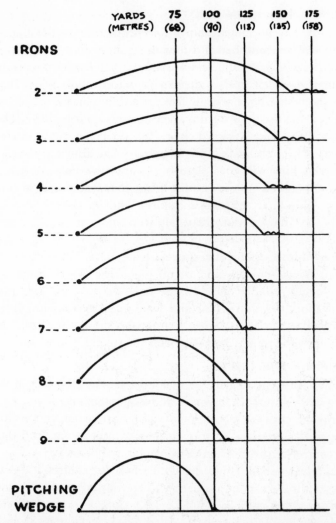

YARDS (METRES)	75 (68)	100 (90)	125 (113)	150 (135)	175 (158)

IRONS

2 - - - -

3 - - - -

4 - - - -

5 - - - -

6 - - - -

7 - - - -

8 - - - -

9 - - - -

PITCHING WEDGE

The higher the number of your iron the greater the loft, and also the less distance you can expect. This chart shows average distances. You can always hit a shorter distance by shortening your swing.

STANCE FOR IRON SHOTS

The square or closed stance (perpendicular to the line of flight) will give you better direction on shots with your 3-iron, as well as with your 1, 2 and 4. Play the ball lined up with the inside of your left heel, and open your feet a little wider than your shoulders. Be sure your feet are firmly planted.

When you use your 5-iron, open up your stance a little. This means that your forward foot (left foot for right-handed player) is brought back of the imaginary line aimed at the pin, and your hips will turn slightly towards the hole. With this half-open stance, you must also bring your feet closer, so they are as wide apart as your shoulders, and be sure they're set firmly on the ground. Play all iron shots from the same position inside your left heel, and not far out.

For a 6-iron, open your stance a trifle more. For the shorter 7-iron, 8-iron, 9-iron, and so on, open the stance more for each higher-number club. In the next chapter, we'll go into detail about the short irons and what you can do with them.

A good rule to remember is this: the shorter the iron the more open the stance, and the closer the spread of your feet.

GRIPPING THE IRON

When we speak of grip, we mean the grip at all points of the swing and not just when you're addressing the ball. If you tend to grip the club too tightly before you start swinging, you are inclined to relax your grip at the top of your swing, and thus lose control of the club on the downswing.

So, take the club firmly in hand when you address the ball with your iron, but don't squeeze. Keep your grip firm throughout your swing, and keep hold of that club as you hit the ball. Obviously you're not going to hit the ball very far if the club is loose in your grasp at impact. But if your grip is firm at that moment, your arms and wrists and everything else will be able to act as part of your unified swing.

It is important that you continue your firm grip right into the follow-through. On iron shots you hit the ground after hitting the ball, and the club will be shaken loose or you'll feel the ground impact if you don't hold a firm grip on the shaft.

Many players like to "choke" an iron a little. I suggest this particularly for golfers under 5 feet 8 (170 cm) or so. The manufacturers make shafts in two lengths—for the tallest normal player and the medium-height one. They expect the shorter player to take his grip lower on the shaft. However, regardless of size, you will be able to get the feel of the club (the flex) better if you choke the iron clubs when you're beginning to play.

DON'T CHANGE YOUR SWING

You will recall that a driver is swung to sweep the ball off the wooden tee. *Never* try to sweep or pick up the ball with an iron! (The "chip" shot is something special, as we'll see in the next chapter.) The face of your iron club is lofted so that you can hit downwards at the back of the ball and send it spinning aloft. You hit down with your irons, just as with the 3-, 4- and 5-woods. Without changing your swing, you hit down and the ball goes up!

Just in case you don't believe this, try an experiment. Take a table-tennis ball and place it on a table. Hold your hand out straight at about the angle of a 7-iron and chop down at the back of the ball with the edge of your palm. What happens? It pops up in the air. Note also that when the ball goes up and forward it also has backspin on it, and bounces back towards your hand if you chop it just right. The same stroke in tennis is called a "chop." This effect in golf is called "pitch" or "backspin."

Every shot you hit with an iron has more or less backspin on

it—or should! Naturally a longer iron will create less backspin than a shorter iron. The 3-iron carries the ball a greater distance and gives it greater roll than a 7-iron, and the 7-iron gives you more backspin.

Let's experiment a little more with the table-tennis ball. If you chop sharply at it, you make it hop up quite a bit. If you hit softly and slowly at it, you can hardly get it up in the air. The same is true with an iron club and golf ball. You must hit sharply at the back of the ball to send it flying!

Not only must you hit sharply but you must catch the back surface of the ball on your downswing. If you hit the ground first you won't be able to chop the ball at all. (If you hit the table before the table-tennis ball, it won't hop.)

Now we know what we want to do with the iron. We want to hit the back surface of the ball as the clubhead swings sharply downward. We know that the ball will spin up from the ground when we do this correctly. But how can you be sure of doing it correctly every time?

I've seen scores of beginners who were under the impression that if they take the right-size divot they'll have the iron shot they want. They concentrate so much on this that they take the divot before they hit the ball. They hit so far in back of the ball that there is hardly any power in their shot. You'll take a divot, true, but if you concentrate on hitting the back of the ball instead of the ground, you'll be much more successful. The divot comes from *in front* of the ball, and your follow-through will automatically take care of it.

(Opposite) When you hit down with your iron, you strike the back of the ball before you touch the ground. This imparts backspin. The divot you take should be shallow, should be from in front of the ball, and should not reduce the power of your shot.

The phases of a full swing. Starting from address (bottom center) the backswing goes to the topswing point (top center). Then the downswing carries you back to the point of impact (bottom center again), and the follow-through is automatic. Note that the arc of the swing is a flattened circle.

So, the first thing is to forget about taking a divot. Look with your left eye at the back of the ball. Try to see a tiny dimple on the ball there and keep it in view all the time you're swinging. You can't hit what you don't see. Watch that dimple on the back of the ball (or the spot where it was) until long after the ball is in flight.

To bring the clubhead smashing into the back of the ball you have to start with your hands in front of the position of the ball. The position at address will be the same for all irons, just slightly in front of the ball.

Start your backswing with the "forward press" (same as with a wood club). You will remember that this is a relaxing action performed by moving your right knee and hands forward towards the line of flight with the clubhead remaining behind the ball. Your next movement is to start the clubhead back from the ball with the feeling of your left forearm's doing the work. Take the clubhead slightly inside of your intended line of flight. Turn your hips as the club goes back.

Your wrists will cock automatically at the top of your swing. Don't even think about the length of your swing, as that will be determined automatically by the length of the club's shaft.

Starting the downswing, you should have the same feeling of the left forearm's pulling the clubhead down. Your shoulders and hips follow the clubhead into the downswing. With each iron, hit down at that spot on the back of the ball. When you get to the hitting area (which is about 12 inches [30 cm] from the ball) then your wrists will automatically uncock and you will hit the ball with the greatest concentration of power.

During the backswing and downswing, your weight will be shifted from (1) a balanced position on the heels of both feet; to (2) weight on your right foot, at the top of your swing; and then quickly to (3) weight on your left foot from start to finish of your downswing. If you shift your weight as in a baseball swing, you'll have no trouble.

You shouldn't have any trouble, either, with your follow-through. The momentum of your swing will cause you to swing right *through* the ball. You can't stop your swing as soon as you hit the ball! The force of your swing should carry the clubhead through as far as the backswing has been. If you take the backswing for a $\frac{3}{4}$ shot with a 9-iron, for instance, you should follow through with a $\frac{3}{4}$ swing. Always try to hold the position of your finish until the ball lands.

The follow-through will hit the ground and you'll take a divot, as I've pointed out. The longer the iron the less divot. You take the divot after you hit the ball, so the divot is just the grass surface which the front of the ball was formerly resting on. If there is a stone in front of your ball, remove it or you'll nick your iron taking the divot. If the stone is not removable, watch out. If your backswing or follow-through may hit a tree or branch, take a practice swing first and see if you can avoid it with a shorter grip and swing.

QUESTIONS ABOUT IRON PLAY

Why do you stand close to the ball on iron shots? Simply to get better control. The shaft is shorter and the iron swing therefore is shorter than your swing with a wood. Your stance is determined by the length of the shaft. If you stand farther away from the ball you have to take a longer and wider swing at it, and then you have to sacrifice accuracy.

Why is the open stance necessary on the shorter irons? When your left side is out of the way, your swing can be more upright, and this allows you to impart more backspin to the ball, thus achieving more accuracy.

Some players tend to swing differently for each different iron shot. This is not only unnecessary but harmful. You will never get your swing established if you have a different groove for each club. There are variations in the amount of strength you put into each shot, of course, and your stance is different under different circumstances, but your swing should be basically the same all the time.

Often, tall players ask me if they should bend over more when they swing an iron. Bending is not a problem if you do everything else as I've outlined it here. Read over and practice the whole section on the stance, grip and swing of the irons, and you'll discover that the length of the club shaft will determine for you the degree of your bend at the hips. A tall player (and clubs are made for tall players) has no real problem. The shorter fellow has to choke his clubs, as I've pointed out, but the big fellow can bend as little as the shaft allows him to.

The arc of the tall player's swing is longer and more abrupt, so that he naturally hits with great loft. The shorter-statured player has more difficulty getting loft. But neither player will have difficulty if he hits sharply at the back of the ball.

Another often-asked question is: why do I get loft and no backspin? The player who asks this usually tells me he hits perfect iron shots at just the right height to land on the green —and then the ball rolls off! The answer is that the seemingly-perfect shots are hit without backspin. This is caused by catching the ball on the upswing, instead of on a sharp downswing. You can recognize when this happens, because no divot is taken at all! The loft is obtained when the slanted clubface lifts the ball. Accuracy in iron play seldom goes hand in hand with "upswing" iron hitters.

One thing I can't repeat frequently enough is to hit *down* with your irons! Good iron play depends on controlling that downswing at the back of the ball. What if you find that you're hitting down sharply, but still you hit the top of the ball? You may be starting with your hands too far out front; or be shifting your weight too far forward on your downswing, causing your hands to draw up at the point of impact with the ball. Look right at the tiny spot on the ball that you want to clip with your club and you'll do it right 99 per cent of the time.

7. The All-Important Short Game

Even more important than the other irons are the short irons—and accuracy with them can be the all-important feature of your game particularly as a young beginner. Once your swing has been established you should concentrate on practicing these "precision shots." No matter what your age, you'll find that you can master the short iron shots after a little effort, and this may give you the opportunity sooner or later of tumbling some hard-driving Goliath from a club championship.

From pro golf tournaments that I've been in, I can quote match after match in which the winner had his short game working for him while the loser was less accurate around the green.

Short iron shots can make or break your game. You are always shooting for the green and the cup with your short approaches. If you land as close as 15 feet (4.5 m) from the cup, you have an excellent chance of sinking your first putt. Even at 20 feet (6 m) you have a good chance. But if you're 25 or 30 feet (7.5 or 9 m) or more from the pin with your short approach, only an excellent or a lucky putt will enable you to trim that one stroke off your score. *Most good players are short-game artists.*

Some beginners confuse pitches and chips, think short shots are soft shots, and tend to smother their short approaches by hitting the ground too hard, or else avoiding backspin pitches entirely. Naturally you don't hit a short approach shot as hard as a longer approach, but you must hit it just as crisply.

There are just two ways you can approach the green from a short distance out:

● by a pitch-and-stop shot (with plenty of backspin), or,

● by a pitch-and-run shot (called a chip shot, if very short).

The method you use is determined by the position your ball is in, and the condition of the green. You use one of the high-loft irons, but exactly which club you select will depend on what you want the ball to do for you.

THE PITCH-AND-STOP

Pitch shots are the best for getting on the green from about 25 yards (23 m) out, or more. If there are obstacles in your way—such as ponds or streams, bunkers or traps, rough or rocks—the only way to get your ball over them is to send it aloft by a pitch shot. Obviously, you can't afford to hit it along the ground, nor should you pitch it on a line the way a baseball pitcher throws a baseball. The "pitch" in golf is the term used for a high shot which makes an arc and lands on the green or at least on the edge of the green.

If the pitch has a great deal of backspin on it, the ball will take a bounce or two and stop. Your aim is to land the ball initially within 10 or 15 feet (3 or 4.5 m) of the cup and make it stop within 3 feet (1 m) or so of the hole. Naturally, you'd like to see the ball drop into the cup (and it does surprisingly often) but you can't count on it. The reason for attempting a

The pitch-and-stop requires a maximum of backspin. Be sure to keep your head down until your chin pushes it up. The divot need not be big. The line of flight here is to the right.

pitch-and-stop shot is that you don't want to take a chance on the way the ball may roll—the green may be on a slant or may be soggy or hard-baked.

For the pitch-and-stop you may use a 9-iron—or, better yet, use a pitching wedge, a club we haven't discussed specially before. The pitching wedge has a high loft, is heavy, and has a large flange to prevent the club from digging too deeply. A beginner can do just about as well with a 9-iron, but after you become experienced you may want to get yourself a wedge too.

With the 9-iron you use a completely open stance, with your

feet close together and your left foot back from the line of flight. (If you use a pitching wedge take the same stance but get even closer.) Face slightly toward the hole. Grip your club 1 inch (25 mm) from the end of the shaft, so that you're choking up on it. Your open stance will make you cock or break your wrists for the backswing more quickly than on the longer approach shots. This makes the backswing almost upright and leads you to make the arc of your downstroke abrupt and vertical too. You again come down hard in back of the ball and you get a tremendous amount of backspin on it.

Don't worry about the divot. If your stroke is right, you take a fairly large but shallow divot in front of the ball and your shot will stop about 10 to 15 feet (3 to 4.5 m) from where it hits the green. If the pin is on the near edge of the green, be sure your pitch-and-stop lands on the grass of the green and not on the apron, even if it means going past the cup a trifle. Always try to land on the green with a pitch shot.

THE PITCH-AND-RUN

For those occasions when the pin is on the back of the green and your ball has a clear space to roll toward the pin, you may prefer to use a pitch-and-run. However, if a green is well-trapped, allowing you only a narrow passage, use the pitch-and-stop shot instead.

If you are from 5 to 20 yards (5 to 18 m) from the green and are clear of encumbrances in your line to the cup, take a 7-iron or 8-iron instead of the club with greater loft. Plan to land the pitch short of the green or on the fringe of it, letting the ball roll the rest of the way to the hole. I use the 8-iron if the pin is in the middle or front of the green, and the 7-iron if it's towards the back and a longer roll is needed.

If you are just off the edge of the green (say, 2 to 10 feet [60 cm to 3 m]) and the pin is another 20 feet (6 m) or so from the edge, use a 6- or 7-iron (never less than a 5-iron) and make a short pitch-and-run, commonly called a "chip shot." I try to choose the club for any type of pitch-and-run by a simple rule: the club has to pitch the ball halfway to the cup and let it roll the rest of the way.

One word of advice about the chip shot: choose the 6 or 7 (maybe even the 5) and stick with it. Don't keep shifting clubs, but use the same one all the time until it becomes second nature to you for that distance, and you'll soon know what to do with it under all circumstances.

Play the pitch-and-run with the same open stance and slight turn towards the hole as in the pitch-and-stop. (Some profes-

The short pitch-and-run (or chip shot) is an arm shot with practically no body or wrist action. For this reason, you play it with an open stance and keep your weight on your left foot. Brush the ball off the ground.

sionals prefer the square stance for the short chip, but I don't get as much accuracy and freedom with it.) The open stance will allow you to *use your arms* without getting any body action into this shot. Keep your weight on your *left* foot and don't try to lift the ball with body or hand movement—let the loft of the club do the trick.

The stroke for the pitch-and-run is quite different from the pitch with backspin. *Don't break your wrists!* Brush the ball off the ground. Let your backswing brush the grass as you bring the clubhead back almost level with the ground, and brush the grass again as you come forward. There is no chance of the ball's stopping where it hits as the spin is forward. If you take a small divot, the run will be cut down slightly. The ball is sure to rise and pitch halfway to the green because you're using a lofted club. This is one of golf's most satisfying strokes when you perform it right.

SHORT IRONS FROM THE TEE

When we first discussed the tee, I pointed out that it's always best to tee up your ball when shooting from the tee. If you hit down in back of the ball, you'll get backspin whether you're on the grass or teed up. You'll get more flight teed up and also more accuracy.

BLASTING FROM A TRAP

The pitching wedge is fine to use for short bunker and sand trap shots (and is very similar to the special "sand wedge"). The flange which prevents your digging too far into the turf on an approach shot likewise prevents your taking too much sand when you use it for blasting or exploding. The high loft of the club allows you to blast high and not too far out of a trap, and land on the green with the maximum of backspin.

The stroke for the blast or explosion shot is the same as for the pitch-and-stop, except that you use less arm power and just

When your ball is buried in sand, it will come out easily if you hit the sand ½ inch (13 mm) in back of the ball and be sure to take a full follow-through. This shot is played with an open stance and hands in front of the ball, so that the clubface is slightly closed.

flick your wrists. Get yourself set with an open stance, with your hands in front of the ball. You should be half-turned towards the pin. Put little body action into the shot, and let your hands, wrists and the heavy clubhead do the work. The length of your backswing will determine how far the ball will travel to reach the green. Take a longer swing from behind a distant bunker than from a deep but just-off-the-green trap. Play the shot firmly and don't be afraid of going too far.

Hit down at a spot exactly one inch (25 mm) in back of the ball on all explosion shots. You don't hit the ball at all! The clubface will dig through the sand behind the ball, and the force of your follow-through will carry the sand and the ball up into the air and down onto the green. So, you can see how important the follow-through is on this shot. If you remember not to scoop at the ball, but stand flat-footed in the sand, you can't help but follow through properly.

If you find it helps, make a slight pivot of your body on the full blast shot to increase the power of your follow-through. The pros do that, especially when there is an overhanging lip on a trap or if the lip is high above your head.

If your ball is buried in the sand, you need to hit closer to the ball—about $\frac{1}{2}$ inch (13 mm) behind it.

RECOVERY SHOTS

Many times there is no need for an explosion shot—you can try a simpler pitch-and-run out of the sand of a shallow trap onto a wide green. This is the same as the fairway pitch-and-run only you have to be doubly certain that you catch the ball

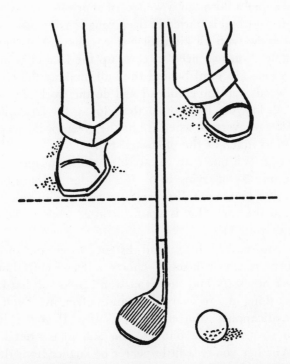

You are not allowed to touch your clubhead to the ground in a sand trap. When lining up, hold your clubhead above the ball and about an inch (25 mm) behind it. Play the ball off your left heel.

first with the opened blade of your 9-iron or pitching wedge, and *not* sand itself in this case. If there is a lip you're not sure of clearing, don't try the pitch-and-run, but blast the ball out.

If the trap is shallow but uphill, you have a different problem. The fact that you must hit the ball up in the air will tend to make you hit harder. This is not necessary, and in fact it will only cause you to push the shot to your right. The trick is to keep the face of your club square to the ball, and this will enable you to control the shot while still giving it loft. You must use either a 9-iron or a wedge, of course.

What if your ball is buried in deep rough? No reason to fret. Golf is a game with all kinds of hazards, but all of them are conquerable. You just need to close up the face of your club and hit $\frac{1}{2}$ inch (13 mm) behind the ball, making the club dig into the weeds and the clubhead will do the work of scooping the ball out for you. Remember that closing the face will give the shot lots of overspin when it hits the green or fairway, and it will run as much as the pitch-and-run.

The wedge is a fine club in capable hands, but most golfers make the mistake of trying to hit the ball too far with it. You cannot try for maximum distance, because the shot will just go higher into the air. This is your "trouble club," the most accurate in your bag.

When you need both loft and distance to get out of a bad spot—in the rough or in sand—choose a longer club than you may think necessary and then you won't press too hard. The important thing in a recovery shot (and in fact, in all golf) is to avoid handicapping yourself unnecessarily. If you're in the woods or rough or in a bunker, you aim to get out in one stroke. Whether you're a little nearer or farther from the pin when you get out is less important than losing a stroke to get in the open. So play it safe. Play it right. Use the right club. Don't try to imitate the professionals. That will come later.

8. Perfection in Your Putting

On the putting green you can reach perfection or near perfection no matter how young you are or how small. Maturity and strength may make a difference when you're trying to drive a ball long and straight down the fairway, but you don't need bulging muscles and terrific strength to roll the ball into the cup.

What you do need is good putting technique. With it you can match your game against a stronger, longer-hitting golfer and still win. Without good putting technique, all your brilliance on the long game or the power game can be nullified once you reach the green. On the other hand, a good putter can get back strokes he has lost in reaching or approaching the green.

THE PUTT IS GOLF'S MOST INDIVIDUAL SHOT

No golfer—amateur or professional—can give you his style of play and say, "That's for you!" Each player is an individual, each player is different. You yourself must find your own style, remembering your particular build and touch.

The putt is golf's most individual shot. You must really experiment, looking for the grip and stance that work best for you. Or, you may find that the one I advocate as "preferred" as a starting point suits you right away. But do your experimenting on the practice greens, not when you're actually playing a round.

When you find a system you think is best for you, stick to it no matter what others may try to tell you about their forms or techniques. The only yardstick of a good putting system is whether your putts are dropping into the cup. If they are, it's a good system, one to stick by.

Don't be like some golfers who keep trying one putting technique after another, even after they have found one that really seems comfortable and profitable. Find a good system and "perfect" it through practice.

No one has ever invented a foolproof way of getting the ball into the cup. That is one of the fascinations of golf.

GET A COMFORTABLE GRIP

There is no such thing as a "standard" putting grip. Anything goes, just as long as you keep sinking your putts.

But there is one grip which is more popular than any other among golf's successful players. This is the reverse overlapping grip used by most professionals. The argument for this type of grip is that it "balances" the two hands, thus helping the clubhead to strike the ball squarely—one of the most important parts of putting.

In the *reverse* overlapping putting grip, the index finger of your left hand should overlap the little finger of your right hand on the shaft. Most of your putting "power" will come from your right hand (provided you're right-handed). Your left hand should be kept under the shaft so that it is the guiding hand. If you do this, you can hinge your wrists in comfort —this is especially important if you are a "wrist" putter, inclined to hit mostly with wrist power.

A faulty grip may cause you some trouble. Gripping the club too tensely leaves no play in your fingers and destroys the sensitive touch so necessary for top-flight putting. So, cultivate a delicate putting grip—firm, but relaxed. If it's the over-lapping grip, fine. If it's your own invention, just make sure it's comfortable for you! No matter what grip you use, always feel comfortable and at ease.

SQUARE OR OPEN STANCE?

There are two basic stances for putting. In the square stance, each foot should be equally distant from the proposed line of roll. In the open stance, your right foot should be closer to the line you want the ball to travel, and your left foot can be farther back, pointed slightly towards the cup or not.

Sometimes I use the square stance but mostly I prefer an open one with my left foot withdrawn from the intended line of roll. I play the ball slightly inside the toe of the left foot and about 3 to 4 inches (75 to 100 mm) from the toe. It is important to play the ball from the same position no matter what break or contour of the green occurs.

Of course, you can also use other stances and perhaps putt just as well. You may prefer to putt with your weight evenly balanced in the center of your stance, or on the right foot. Experiment and see what is most comfortable and natural for you.

Whatever your stance, play the ball close to your feet and keep your head *directly* over the ball and the top of your putter blade. If you have your feet too close together or too wide, or if your head is not centered, you can be thrown off balance by the smallest thing—even a slight wind.

YOUR PUTTING STROKE

In putting you bend both elbows, and you have a choice of three arm movements. You may keep your arms close to your body. You may point your left elbow towards the cup. Or, you may prefer the wrist system I use, which is to confine your arm movement and let your wrists move the clubhead.

As you keep your eyes directly above the top of your club-head, size up the ball. Make sure that the face of your putter is at a right angle to the line along which you want the ball to travel. Let's assume that you have already "read" the green and obtained the line of roll in your mind's eye.

When you are ready to putt, take the club back smoothly (with your wrists mainly) making sure you keep the clubface square to the line. Keep the blade low to the ground at all times.

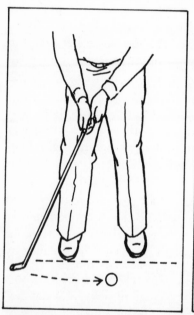 

(Left) Take the putter back smoothly, without rolling your wrists, but keeping the clubhead close to the ground. (Right) If your wrists do their work properly, your putter will swing like a pendulum, and hit the ball solidly on long or short putts.

The shorter your backstroke the less chance of error. Don't take the putter back too far. If you do, it will cause you either to swing too hard, or to slow down your swing as you realize this fact. Hesitation anywhere in the swing usually destroys the smoothness you need for successful putting. If you let your wrists do the work and restrict your backswing, you'll get a sharper impact and more accuracy.

Follow through about the same distance from the ball's original position as you take on your backswing. In other words, let the clubhead make a pendulum swing. Keep the clubface at a right angle to the path of the ball, even after impact.

When the stroke is like a pendulum, your wrists can remain fixed over the ball and hinge back and forth. You may prefer to have your wrists remain solid, so that you give the ball a "push." I find the solid-wrist push type of putt fine on short putts but hard to control on putts over 30 feet (9 m). So, I try to get a combination of the two.

The important thing about stroking a putt is to find a method which makes you hit the ball solid every time. Practice until you get that.

LINING UP YOUR PUTT

We have gone through all the mechanics of putting. Now for some "inside" tips that should help you develop into a top-flight putter.

My tried-and-true way of lining up a putt is to start out by aiming off to the left of the hole and then gradually I turn my putter back to the line of the putt. In this way I keep my stance open and have the feeling of hitting *out* and along my line. I always try to imagine the line my ball will travel along.

Keep your putter aiming at the hole when there is no break in the green that causes you to line up differently. Keep your eye on the *back* of the ball.

You probably have seen players "soling" their putters without even realizing that's what they were doing. This is the technical term for the almost unconscious act of a great majority of golfers who place their putter blade in front of the ball, then sight along the imaginary path they want their putt to follow, before bringing the putter back in back of the ball in position for their swing.

The idea is that this automatic screening of the ball helps to pin-point the intended line of the putt. If it helps you, "sole" your putter. But you must be careful not to touch the ball and to keep the clubhead at a right angle to the putting line both in front of the ball and again when you lift the club into position behind the ball. The putter face must be perpendicular to the proposed line of roll to insure a true putt. Even a slight mistake on what consitutes a right angle will mean an off-line putt.

A way of checking the squareness of your blade is to step a pace to your right and put the putter down inches (centimetres) in back of the ball. Follow through towards the cup without touching the ball. Check your aim and polish your follow-through. Make sure you're lined up right. Remember, the cup is only 4 inches (100 mm) wide, so if you're not exactly right on angle, you'll be an inch or two (25 or 50 mm) off line and may lose a valuable stroke.

DON'T LIFT YOUR HEAD WHEN PUTTING!

After estimating the distance you will have to putt, imagining the line the ball should follow, and squaring your clubhead to that line, look at the back of the ball. Concentrate solely on the ball! Don't look up to watch the cup or the ball's progress after impact. In fact, don't look up until you're sure the ball has either dropped into the cup or has stopped rolling.

Looking up is a serious fault in all golf strokes, but it's fatal in putting. Topping a putt is as easy as topping a 3-wood shot.

Keep your mind completely on the ball and your swing. Stroke the ball smoothly and crisply—don't jab at it! Make sure not to move your shoulders, hips or head.

Do everything according to plan, and when you look up that ball will usually be in the cup!

At first you may have difficulty judging the distance your putts must travel, and consequently you may encounter trouble in judging the force you need behind the clubhead. Unfortunately, there is no standard rule or easy way of learning this —it's a problem that can be overcome only by experience and hours of steady practice.

Putting short is a common fault among young golfers, and among average golfers of all ages. It's caused either by head lifting, by an overly slow swing or by too much hesitation at some point in the swing. Always putt *strongly enough* for the ball to roll past the cup a little bit if it misses. If it doesn't reach the cup, it can't roll in. A putt that's hit just a little too hard may well strike the back rim of the cup and fall in—especially when you least expect it!

"Feel" plays the major role in helping you gauge the strength of each of your putts. I can't define "feel" but you'll know when you attain it. Keep your grip relaxed, but putt firmly, and soon you'll get the feel of putting.

HOW TO JUDGE A GREEN

You can "read" a golf green almost as you read a book. In looking at a green's surface, watch for rises and depressions in the ground. When you putt, you must compensate for rolls to the right or left. Every green has some roll. Look for it, and take it into consideration when you putt. If the section of the green between your ball and the cup slopes even slightly from right to left, for example, you must not attempt to putt on a straight line. Try it and you'll see that on such a green the ball will roll past the cup on the left side. Therefore, in this case, you would putt slightly to the right, and the roll of the green will carry the ball into the cup.

After getting down on one knee and noting the slope, you should look over the entire line your ball will take to the cup. Look from both sides of the hole. Many golfers fail to do this. Your object is to judge how much speed the ball needs to roll up to and drop into the cup. If the grass is short or the ground well pressed down, you can figure that it's a "fast" green and a gentle roll will keep the ball in motion until it reaches the cup. If the grass is long or the ground is soft, you can figure the area is "slow" and you'll need to give your putt more power.

In general, fast greens are usually dry, hard-packed or sun-baked surfaces, "*with* grain" (we'll explain this in a moment), or they are closely mowed or recently mowed. Slow greens may be slow because you're putting against the grain or because the grass has been permitted to grow too long, or because of early morning dew, heavy rains the night before or recent watering by the greenskeeper's assistant. The soggier the green the slower it is.

THE "GRAIN" OF THE GREEN

Not only must you note the green's speed, but you should also note the direction of the grass's "grain." This may sound mysterious, but it's simply the direction in which the grass is growing. It's a lot like the nap on your living room rug (which, incidentally, is a good place to practice your putting).

The easiest way to tell the grain of a green is to look towards the cup and notice if there is a shine on the grass. If you see a shine, it means the grass is growing away from you and you will be putting *with* the grain. In this case, your putt will travel farther with less effort on your part. Don't hit the ball too hard or you'll overshoot the cup when you putt with the grain.

Naturally, if you see no shine, it means you are putting against the grain, and you must use a little extra effort to make

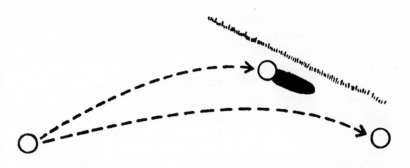

On a sidehill putt, you must hit slightly uphill so the slope of the green can carry your ball into the cup. If you putt straight, the slope will carry your putt off line. Putting with speed will not help.

your putt reach the cup. Get down on one knee and look carefully if you're not sure you see a shine.

Sometimes as you look towards the cup you will notice that the shine shows only on one side or the other. This means that you will be putting *across* the grain at an angle. For example, if you see the grass shine only on your right, you can be sure the grain is from left to right. Therefore, your putt may be swung from left to right a little, just as if the ground sloped a trifle that way. You must compensate for this by putting slightly to the left. Of course, you do just the opposite if the shine is on the other side.

Try a few cross-grain putts the next time you're on the practice green and you'll soon see how to play the ball.

I've often been asked what to do if the grain is from left to right and the ground slopes from right to left. If you think that one will offset the other exactly, you putt straight away. If the slope is severe, you must compensate for that and forget about the grain. Just how much the grain affects your putt depends on the length of the grass too. A slow or heavy green will give you more grain than a short-cropped playing surface.

Through trial and error you will become an expert on grains.

PUTTING UPHILL AND DOWN

When putting uphill, you should grasp your clubhandle more firmly than on flat surfaces and hit the ball so it will carry about 6 to 8 inches (15 to 20 cm) past the cup if you miss. The missed putt may roll back a little (even into the cup!) if the hill is steep.

Most players consider downhill putting harder. Your grip should be more relaxed—not weak, however. Be careful not to hold the putter *too* loosely. Hit the ball more on the toe of the putter. Gravity will help you get the ball down to the cup. Never putt downhill to be short, as the easier putt is an uphill one.

BE PATIENT AND PRACTICE

Good putting will reward you with good scores. The ability to read greens and putt successfully seems to elude many golfers but you can master it with practice and study. The only way to study putting is to get out on the green and meet the different conditions, recognize them, and practice your putting until you are able to compensate for any roll or grain. There is no substitute for actual play when you know what you're doing.

When you get out on the green, remember what you've read here. Take your time. Read the green. Size up your putt—each putt. Don't be afraid to get down on your hands and knees for a better look. Study the line between your ball and the cup from behind your ball. Then look at it from behind the cup itself. Stand back and see how far you have to putt.

Don't be rushed! The hurried shot, and especially the hurried putt, usually finishes yards (metres) off the target. I know. Learn patience and concentration.

DON'T CONCEDE A THING!

A last point I'd like to dwell on is the recognized but regrettable practice of conceding putts.

"Oh, it's such a short one," you'll hear average golfers say, "you'll make it. You concede mine and I'll concede yours." And they pick up their balls.

Is it any wonder their putting doesn't improve when they concede putts? That's why average putters stay average.

You should lose no opportunity to hole out, to drop that ball into the cup no matter how short the putt is. That's the object of the whole game. Another thing is that every successful putt increases your self-confidence. You develop a "feel" for putting by dropping the short ones. They're just as important and count just the same as the long ones.

You can't concede in a tournament, so if you hope some day to be a tournament winner (amateur or professional) you'll have to sink every putt. The "conceders" are the ones who have nightmares of missing a putt they should have made!

Practice regularly, putt every chance you get, concede not even the simplest of putts, and you are headed for brilliant play on the greens.

9. Let's Play a Few Holes

Now you've learned the swing and each type of stroke, and you're ready to start out on the golf course. I'll go along a few holes with you to see what happens.

FIRST HOLE—374 YARDS (337 M)—PAR 4

You walk up to the tee and notice that the fairway slopes away from tee to green. You know this means your ball will roll downhill when it lands and you'll get extra distance. You don't have to get the ball so high up in the air as you might if you were facing level ground or an upslope. For this reason, you choose your driver to drive with.

You take the ball in the palm of your hand and the tee, point out, between your fingers. You press the tee into the ground (using the ball to push it with) at a point midway between the tee markers. You set the ball about one finger's height from the ground.

Now you address the ball so that your left heel is lined up with the ball, and your line of flight is aimed directly at the flag on the green. You settle your feet, and take your grip. Without hurrying you go into your swing, a full swing, hitting the ball squarely in the back and sweeping it away with overspin. You follow through, still keeping your head down. The ball zooms upwards. . . .

When you look up you see the ball landing on the fairway about 180 yards (162 m) out. It takes one long bounce, then some shorter ones and finally settles about 210 yards (189 m) from the tee, more than halfway to the green.

After the other players shoot, you walk out on the fairway to your ball. The grass is fairly heavy and that is why your ball rolled only 30 yards (27 m) although it was running downhill. You are now approximately 165 yards (149 m) from the green. Which club should you choose? Your 3-iron will give you a minimum of 165 yards (149 m) (you know from your distance chart), and your 5-iron will have to be strongly hit to go that far. However, you're shooting downhill and this makes the air distance shorter. Because of this and because the grass is thick around your ball, you choose the higher-loft 5-iron.

DOWNHILL LIE

If you were playing this shot from a perfectly level lie, you would use a half-open stance, with your left foot slightly back from the line of flight and your feet spread almost as wide as your shoulders. However, when you take this stance you notice that your left foot is downhill, below the level of the ball. This should make you stop and think.

You realize that the arc of your downswing will hit the ground before it hits the ball, unless you adjust your stance. What do you do for a downhill lie? You spread your feet a little farther apart (to bring the central point of the arc farther forward) and you also move your feet farther forward (so that the ball is played nearer your right foot). This assures your hitting the ball first, instead of the ground. You can now hit down at the back of the ball and you will take a divot *after* you hit the ball. You can't shift your weight too far onto your right foot in the backswing, because your left foot will rise from the turf and you'll lose balance. Therefore, you must keep your weight from shifting too much, especially before impact.

All right. You know what you want to do. You do it. After impact you clip the ground with your iron, and you end with most of your weight on your left foot in the follow-through. The ball doesn't go too high (not as high as it would if hit from level ground) but it makes a neat loop and bounces on the apron of the green. It hops up a couple of times, then rolls fairly rapidly (not much backspin) and heads for the back edge of the green. Will it stop? It does—right on the short grass edge!

CHIPPING UP

When your foursome reaches the green, you take a look at your lie. It's in fairway grass (not on the smooth grass of the green) and just behind your ball is quite-high grass (through which your club will swish). You decide to chip the ball up to the cup with your 7-iron. This will be a pitch-and-run shot, so you want to land the ball on the fly half the distance to the pin. You're 20 feet (6 m) away from the pin, so you want to loft the ball 10 feet (3 m) and roll another 10 feet (3 m).

With your trusty 7-iron (the club you use to chip with) you take a fully open stance. Your left foot is back and your body is turned slightly towards the cup. You keep your weight on your left foot, and concentrate on the ball. You must hit it cleanly and with just enough power. You come back with your clubhead through the fairly heavy grass, using only your arms. You don't break your wrists or pivot your body at all. You need to stroke the ball with very little power. Your club seems to brush the ball off the ground. It hops up above the medium-high grass, bounces on the green and rolls. It trickles along towards the cup but, sad to say, not in exactly a straight line. It goes past the cup, and stops more than 2 feet (60 cm) away, to the right of the pin.

PUTTING FOR PAR

If you sink this putt, you'll have a par 4. You really want to sink it.

What's the first thing you do? You go far in back of your ball (say 15 feet or 4.5 m), get your head down near the level of the green, and see if the ground rolls at all. It does. It rolls just a trifle to the left. That's why your ball stopped where it did. You didn't notice the roll before. Now you know what to do—you'll putt for the right side of the cup and gravity will pull the ball to the left and into the cup. To judge the distance, you take another look from near the pin.

You take your comfortable putting stance (square or open, whichever you prefer) and get your eyes directly above the ball. You line up the putt with the cup's right edge by "soling" your putter in front of the ball perpendicular to that imaginary line. Then you lift the putter back behind the ball. You see the line in your mind's eye. Back you draw your putter with your wrists, and slowly you bring it forward. You want to hit the ball only about 2½ feet (75 cm) at most—no more than 6 inches (15 cm) past the cup if you miss.

You make a slow graceful arc with your putter. You tap the ball squarely in the back. The ball heads for the right edge of the cup. Is it too far off line? It seems to be. Oh, now it's slowing down and curving left. It teeters on the lip of the cup, and then plunk! It drops out of sight with that delightful sound of a sunk putt ringing in your ears. You have your first par!

Wasn't that easy?

SECOND HOLE—523 YARDS (471 M)—PAR 5

As you walk to this tee, you see that although the tee itself is built up on a mound above the ground, the fairway rises in the distance and you can't see the green, which is far away and past the horizon. Moreover, right in front of the tee for about 60 yards (54 m) is heavy rough.

Your tee shot will need greater loft than on the previous hole and it won't roll very far uphill when it lands. For this reason, you are tempted to choose your 3-wood because it will give

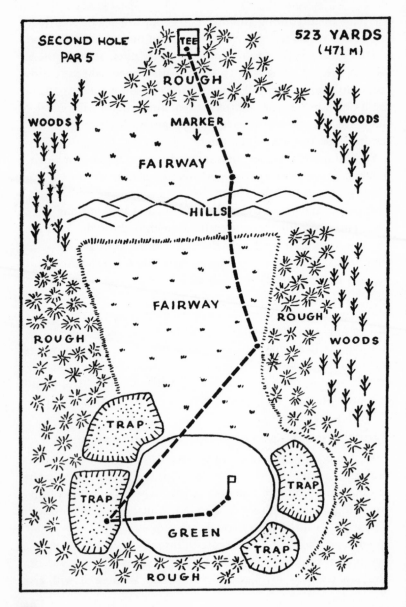

SECOND HOLE
PAR 5

523 YARDS
(471 M)

ROUGH

TEE

MARKER

WOODS

WOODS

FAIRWAY

HILLS

FAIRWAY

ROUGH

ROUGH

WOODS

TRAP

TRAP

TRAP

GREEN

TRAP

ROUGH

96

you enough loft and a little greater distance on this long hole.

You tee up your ball two fingers high, not pressing the tee as far into the turf. You'll need all the help you can get to get the ball up and soaring. If you hit a little under the ball, it will be better than topping it.

You take your stance as for a drive (which this is) even though you are using your 3-wood. You get your line of flight from the fairway direction marker 100 yards (90 m) out, and again without hurrying you start your swing. You pivot, take a full backswing, cock your wrists, hesitate at the top point, come down with increasing speed and power, snap your wrists squarely into the hitting area, and sock! After impact, with your head still down, you let the momentum carry you through, and your right shoulder brings up your head.

The ball shot out for perhaps 30 yards (27 m) before it started really rising, your friends tell you. When you yourself first catch sight of the ball, it's way up in the air, headed a little to the left of the direction marker and still going at good speed. It loses height and speed now and drops to the ground, takes only three bounces and stops rolling. But it's way out there, about 200 yards (180 m) or more.

UPHILL LIE

When you reach your ball, you find you can't yet see the green. But by walking ahead another 25 yards (23 m) to the top of the rise, you get a glimpse of the green, still 300 yards (270 m) away. Marking a spot on the rise for line-up, you go back to your ball. The grass is not heavy, but you have to shoot uphill and clear the top of the rise to get good distance. So you decide on your 3-wood.

Ordinarily you would play the ball from the inside of your left heel when you use the 3-wood. But with an uphill lie, how can you adjust your stance? You stop and figure it out.

Your left foot is going to be above the level of the ball and this will tend to make the arc of your swing uphill, passing over the top of the ball. So you bring back your left foot to line up the toe with the ball (just about as in the driving stance), but you don't spread your feet apart quite as far.

Now you get set, take your swing and come neatly into the back of the ball. You take a small divot even though you could not hit down on the ball. (The tilt of the ground makes you do it.) The ball rises rapidly, because of the loft of your 3-wood, clears the rise and then, instead of keeping on a straight line towards the green, it veers a little to the left. Why? Because you were still hitting uphill, and the tendency was to pull (or hook) the ball to your left.

But no matter. You got good distance, and you're not too far off line.

When you reach your ball, however, you see that there's a problem. You have at least 175 yards (158 m) still to go, because you've added to the distance by going off line, and you're just in the rough.

OUT OF THE ROUGH

Your first question is what club to use. You must reach the green with the next shot, and it's possible for you to do it with either your 4-wood or your 3-iron (you don't carry a 2-iron). But perhaps a 5-iron would be safer because you're in the rough. You discard this idea, as the rough is sparse and thin, and the loft of either of the other clubs is likely to get you out with ease. However, the 3-iron will be the safer club, so you choose that.

When you take your square stance with the 3-iron, you find that both your feet are a little higher than the ball. In other words, you have a "sidehill lie." Be sure you get close enough, so that you're not reaching for the ball. Now instead of playing the ball from the inside of your left heel, you play it a little farther back, towards your right foot. The tendency is to slice from this position of feet-above-ball, but you're already off the fairway to the left, and a slice will help you get back on line.

So you shoot as you are, aiming to the left of your target. You take a full swing with your 3-iron, hit down at the back of the ball, and get a beautiful shot away! The divot is small and the ball turns slightly to the right. Down it comes with backspin on the right side of the green, away from the pin, and suddenly it disappears. Where has it gone? Into a sand trap.

It was a good shot, but you're in trouble. That's golf.

OUT OF SAND

Don't bemoan your fate. Blasting out of a sand trap is one of golf's easiest shots, and one of the most picturesque.

You discover your ball in ribbed sand, which is light and not clayey. The trap is not very deep, and the lip is only about level with your shoulders. This is a fine opportunity to use a pitching wedge. The heavy clubhead with its great loft will lift the ball right out of the sand, and it won't travel too far. You have only 50 feet (15 m) to the pin. A short explosion shot will do the trick.

You address the ball without touching your clubhead to the sand! Just hold the club in position behind the ball and above it about 1 inch (25 mm). Get your feet set flat in the sand with an open stance after you have a line on the pin. You want to hit down at a spot just 1 inch (25 mm) behind the ball. You decide to take a shortened swing, coming back only up to waist level, and cocking your wrists at that point.

Ready now. You take the club back easily, cock your wrists, and start your downswing, gaining speed rapidly but not putting much body action into the shot. You keep your feet flat. This is mostly a wrist shot. You snap your wrists just before "impact," which really isn't impact at all because you won't hit the ball—just flick through the sand about an inch (25 mm) in back of the ball. Your follow-through carries the sand and ball with high loft up onto the green. Your ball hits the sod of the green with a sound plunk, bounces a few feet (a metre) and stops just about 8 feet (2.5 m) short of the pin. You lie 4. Still a chance for par.

PUTTING AGAINST THE GRAIN

This putt is important. If you can sink it, you have a par 5—after being in all kinds of trouble!

You take your time about looking over the green. You squat in back of the ball, remove some twigs from your line of putt, go to the other side of the flag and note how far away the cup really is. What else do you see? You see a slight uphill roll towards the cup, so you know you'll need a little more steam behind your putt than if the green were level. Also, you see the grain is against you—there is no shine on the grass as you look towards the cup, but a furriness like the roughened surface of a carpet. You'll have to hit with even more power on this fairly short putt. "Never up, never in" runs through your mind. If you don't get *up* to the cup, your putt won't drop.

So, carefully, you take your stance. You "sole" your club to get exactly the right line. It's almost straightaway. You aim to stop about 6 inches (15 cm) past the cup if you miss. But this doesn't mean that you're going to take a long backswing. On the contrary, you will swing back only about 12 inches (30 cm), and will use your wrists for power.

You're set. You putt easily, letting the clubhead do the work, but keeping a tight grip on the shaft. You have your eye on a back dimple of the ball. You click the putt away. It's a little too strong! But it's straight and it hits the back of the cup. It hops a little in the air, then comes down again on the backlip, hesitates and then falls neatly into the hole. You're in! You've done it! Two pars in a row.

THIRD HOLE—145 YARDS (131 M)—PAR 3

The par-5 hole was where you were supposed to relax. This short hole is a tough one! But nothing fazes a good golfer. It's your honor again.

Really a beauty of a hole, this requires a pitch-and-stop tee shot from a low level, across a small pond to a sharply-banked green set like a diamond in the middle of yawning sand traps. To make things just a little sportier, there are weeping willow trees part-way around the pond, with only a small opening between them which a low shot might or might not clear.

The safest way to play this tee shot is *over* the treetops. If you hit the shot well, loft and backspin will help you stick to the sloping green. If you're not quite straight, you'll still clear the trees with a high shot. On the other hand, if you attempt a lower pitch shot (with say a 5-iron) you might not stick to the green even if you go through the passage in the trees. You could use a 5-iron and still loft it over the trees, but you're most certain of loft with your 7-iron. Well hit, a 7-iron shot will easily travel the 145 yards (131 m) to the pin, especially if you tee up the ball a bit.

You've completely forgotten about the pond. It might as well be level land as water—you're going to fly right over it no matter what.

You take your open stance, and play the teed-up ball off the heel of your left foot. You'll hit down on the ball, probably won't take a divot of any size, and the loft of the club will send the ball shooting up with backspin.

You settle your feet firmly, address the ball, then come back in a full swing. Down come your arms, snap go your wrists, and you've hit the ball solidly right in the back. Your club just scrapes the ground as you follow through.

When you look up your ball is well above the trees. Will it go over the green? No, it only seems that way. It catches the slope of the green to the left of the pin, bounces almost straight up in the air, then rolls in a looping curve towards the edge of a trap. But no, it doesn't go in.

You're the only player who pitched to the green. You see your ball perched up on the topmost point of the green, and downhill to your left is the pin, some 35 feet (about 11 m) away. You go behind the pin then, and see that your ball will have to describe a wide curve, way off to the left, along the edge of the trap, and then break towards the cup at the last moment in order to go in. It's a long putt and a difficult one.

When it's your turn to putt, you go to your ball and envision the line the putt should take. You want to pass the cup if you miss, so your next putt will be uphill and thus easier. You grasp the shaft with a relaxed but not loose grip and swing with your wrists. The ball seems to trickle along the edge of the trap. Will it ever curve down? Yes, there it goes, heading down the slope now as if another hand were guiding it. You hit it to the left, and now it's rolling to the right! But it started to curve just a little too soon.

As it heads down, you realize that it's short of the cup by a good bit.

Your next putt will be downhill again on this sloping green. This time, though, it will be a short putt—about 3 feet (1 m). The others have putted out when you take your stance. It's easy. But you take just as much care with this short putt as you did with the long one. A careless putt can hike your score way up.

Smoothly and confidently, you stroke the ball with your relaxed grip, aiming again a little to the left. The ball comes around beautifully into the wide mouth of the cup, and plunks to the bottom of the cup. It's music to your ears! Three pars in a row. Yes, golf can be as easy as that.

10. How to Practice and Think Golf

You wouldn't think of going out to play a baseball game without warming up. First, you loosen up your muscles, then practice a few swings, and finally you put on some steam after getting control of the bat and the ball.

In the same way, you should never go out on the golf course without practicing first. You will certainly need to practice a few putts, and I suggest that you start on the practice green. Take your time "getting your eye" and swinging rhythmically with your putter. How long should you stay on the green? That depends on you and your condition and ability—from 5 minutes to a half-hour.

From the practice green, you should go to a pitching area. Here you can practice with your 7-iron and 9-iron or pitching wedge. Take it easy. Don't sock the ball hard, but try to get your timing perfected. Line up your shots and aim for a certain spot to test your accuracy. Practice with four or five balls, battered practice balls, but round ones! To practice with a cut-up ball that doesn't fly or roll straight will do you no good. Try some explosion shots from sand, if you have the chance.

Don't even hold a wood in your hands until your muscles are limbered up from your putting and pitching. If there is a practice tee on your course, go there and hit a dozen or so balls. If not, take a number of swings with your woods in the fairway practice area, using a cloth ball if you have one. Always *aim at something*—a piece of paper, a coin, anything as small as a golf ball or smaller. If you use a practice ball or cotton ball, tee it up now, and try a few drives. Then you're ready to go out on the course.

THE PSYCHOLOGY OF GOLF

People tell you to be confident—that you need the right psychology to play a good game of golf. There's a lot to that, but what many people forget to mention is that confidence without ability is impossible to maintain. You can't feel confident very long if you don't know how to hit the ball. You can't start golf on the first tee, armed only with confidence, and expect to drive the ball 200 yards (180 m). You won't. (In fact, you may not even hit the ball.) However, once you've learned to play golf and have the proper swing, you'll have the right to self-confidence.

What is the "right psychology" in golf? It's the "feeling of the mind" which tells you that you're going to make a wonderful shot. You'll be surprised how often you will! If you feel "in your mind" that you'll sink your putt, you have a better chance of sinking it.

The confident frame of mind will help you through bad spots. If at times you make a bad shot, you needn't lose confidence. Just stop and say something like this to yourself: "That shot was bad, but I've made good shots in exactly that situation, and I can make many more good ones. The next shot will give me a chance to recover what I lost." You know this is true, and your confidence returns when you prove this point to yourself. If you also prove your ability to others, that's fine, but it's less important. The main thing, unless you're playing golf exhibitions, is to show *yourself* you can make any shot in golf.

With that in mind, you can go confidently from shot to shot. No false confidence, but a sure, relaxed frame of mind, free of negative thoughts, anxieties or worries about your game, is what you need to play golf. You don't need lessons in psychology. Your game, if it's good, will give you all you need.

WHAT THE PRO CAN'T TEACH YOU

No one can give you lessons in consistency. The pro can show you how to play particular shots, and this book too can prepare you for every occasion, but no one can teach you consistency. That is up to you. Remember this: the earlier in life you start golf, the better chance you have of playing a consistently good game. By starting golf young, you're learning at a time when your mind and muscles are most receptive. You learn a series of movements which does not contradict anything you learned before. You're starting with a clean slate, and the golf history you write on it will be your own.

You may record a long series of high-scoring rounds at the start. But you should start bringing your score down by dint of hard work and practice. Be honest with yourself each time you post your score. If one day you are beaten by a friend, don't let it rankle. Just compare your scores with your previous scores, and try to improve consistently.

Come back to this book often and check yourself and your swing. Make sure you're doing the right thing, hitting the ball properly, taking your time, and all the rest of it. Try to remember what each club is supposed to do for you. You'll soon find it comes as second nature to you to select the right club, and use it in the right way. If you're not sure, look in the book.

Consistency of performance is what you're after. You want each shot to travel straight and true. You want each pitch to hit the green with backspin. You want each putt to drop, not just a majority of them. Of course, you won't reach perfection, but you must try for it! When you fall short, be realistic enough not to let it upset you. Just count how close to perfection you've come.

Another thing to remember about consistency is this: you can't afford to take chances. You must play each shot the safe way to get a consistently good score. In a match, it's a different thing—you might as well lose a hole by two strokes as by one. But in ordinary friendly play (and it's mostly medal play, total score), you play to avoid errors and that means playing safely. Judgment goes hand in hand with consistency.

THINK OF THE OTHER FELLOW

Etiquette is important to a consistent game. How? If you do something that isn't allowed by the rules (and you offend yourself as well as your fellow players when this happens), then you're bound to play for a while in a disturbed frame of mind. Your relaxed, confident feeling will disappear in thin air.

But abide by the rules, be fair to your opponents and to the players in front of you and behind you, think of their feelings, lean over backwards to give them the benefit of every doubt, and you'll be playing with a clear mind—you'll be thinking good golf.

Certainly your game is important. That's why you play golf —to get enjoyment from playing correctly—but the other fellow's game is just as important, and you shouldn't spoil it. Learn the rules of golf (some time later you can learn the tournament rules) and keep them in mind whenever you're out on the course. You'll find them written simply in the next chapter. When there is a disagreement between players, show them the rules in the book and you'll settle all arguments. I can't stress too much the need to avoid disputes and keep golf the friendly game it's meant to be. It's up to you.

11. Rules for a Friendly Game
(including Etiquette)

Many golfers play the game for years without learning the rules. You don't have to be a stickler for the rules in a friendly game—it won't be friendly if you are—but you should know what the rules are in order to avoid embarrassing situations and the formation of bad habits. You should learn the rules for all the commonest situations and you should understand the reasoning behind them so that you can make and follow your own course or group rules when you have a friendly game.

Tournament rules are very specific. They were originally written by lawyers and are naturally in legal language. The interpretations made from time to time by the United States Golf Association and the Royal and Ancient Golf Club of St. Andrews (the British golf authority) are explanatory, if you understand the legal language. What follows in this chapter is an interpretation of the official rules in non-legal language, with variations that should be allowed in a friendly medal game or match. In a tournament, you must adhere closely to the official rules of that tournament. When you enter, find out the tournament rules and stick to them!

In the meantime, learn the everyday rules and follow them:

1. INTERFERENCE. When a player is shooting, no one should talk or move or allow his shadow to fall across the ball or the immediate area. No one should stand close to the player or ball, or get in the line of vision of the player. For your own protection, don't stand directly behind the player shooting, or you may get hit with the club. Of course, you should never stand where you can get hit with the ball. Stand slightly behind and to the right.

2. PRACTICE SHOTS. Practice swings are permissible if you do not swing anywhere near a teed-up ball or a ball in play. (If you whiff, count it a stroke and not a practice swing.) You may not take a practice stroke with a ball, nor roll a ball by hand across the green, for instance, to determine the roll or grain. After everyone has putted out, you may want to take a practice putt to see what you did wrong, and this is permissible if no one behind you is waiting to play to the green.

3. PRIORITY ON THE COURSE. If your match (or foursome) fails to keep its place on the course, and falls more than a clear hole behind the players in front, then you should allow a match or foursome behind you to go through if they want to. A twosome ("single match") naturally plays faster than a foursome, and should have the right to go through a slow foursome or threesome.

4. PLAYING THROUGH. Players looking for a lost ball should allow other matches coming up to play through. Once the signal is given to go through, step to the side of the fairway. If the lost ball is found in the meantime, you must not continue play and try to keep your place—but must allow the group going through to play and go ahead.

5. WAITING TO HIT. Never hit a ball until the party in front of you is completely out of range (not just your normal range but the range of a professional). When it is your chance to shoot, hit the ball without undue delay. Don't fidget around. When you have holed out, step off to the side of the green to tally your scores as players may be behind you. (Do this even if they aren't.)

6. THE HONOR. On the first tee, draw lots for the honor of shooting first. After this, the winner of the hole (or winning team) should have the honor on the next tee. If the hole is halved (tied), then the player who had the honor retains it. The sequence on the tee should be by low score—in other words, the player with the next to lowest score shoots second, etc. Only one player should tee up his ball at a time. Don't stand near the front of the tee, or leave your ball anywhere on the tee while another is shooting.

7. STANCE. When you tee up, you may stand with your feet outside the teeing area, but your ball must be inside it. For instance, one foot may be in front of the line. You are not allowed to build a stance for yourself when taking a tee shot or any shot. You can dig your spikes into the ground the way a baseball player does. You may settle yourself firmly without kicking up any dirt or grass.

8. TEE MISPLAYS. If your ball falls off the tee it may be re-teed without penalty. If you tap the ball off the tee while addressing, it may be re-teed according to U.S.G.A. rules, without penalty.

9. ADVICE. Take advice only from your caddie and don't offer advice to another player. This is not only an official rule in a tournament, but a rule of etiquette in a friendly game. If you know the course, and another player doesn't, tell him the layout of the hole, but don't tell him what club to take, or how to swing or putt.

10. SCORE INFORMATION. When another player in your match (or foursome) asks you how many strokes you have taken up to a certain point, tell him. You want him to tell you, too. This may influence you in taking a chance or not, for instance, in playing the hole.

11. LINE OF PLAY. If you want to know the line of play, such as where the green beyond the hill is, or where the pin is on the green, ask your caddie to tell you, or to hold up the flagstick so you can see it.

12. HITTING. You are not allowed to push, drag, scrape or spoon the ball—you have to stroke it! This goes particularly for short putts, and sand shots.

13. LIES. You must play the ball from wherever it lies. If you are in soft or high grass or deep sand, you have to play it. (There are special rules for unplayable lies, which you will find in No. 29.) If you are in a divot hole, you must play the ball without touching it. You can now see the importance of replacing divots you make on the fairway.

14. PRIORITY IN PLAY. The player whose ball is farthest from the hole plays first, after you have all teed off. If two players are equidistant, either player may shoot. One exception in a friendly game is around the green: the player who is off the green shoots before any player on the green shoots (even if the latter is farther from the cup). This is not the case in a tournament.

15. **DROPPING A BALL.** When you have to drop a new ball (replacing a lost ball), drop it nearest to the spot where you think it was lost. The ordinary procedure for dropping is to stand erect facing the hole, and drop the ball behind you over your shoulder. If the ball twice rolls nearer the hole (because of a slope), place the ball, instead of dropping it.

16. **TOUCHING THE BALL.** You are not allowed to touch a ball while it is in play, with any part of your body. You may touch the ball while addressing it, provided you don't move it or knock it off the tee. You may pick up a ball to identify it, but you must then replace it in the exact spot.

17. **BALL HITS BALL.** If your ball hits and moves an opponent's ball, he has the choice of leaving it where it lies or replacing it as near as possible to the spot from which it was moved. For instance, if you hit an opponent's ball with your ball and it rolls nearer the green, he can leave it there. If it rolls into a trap, he may remove it without penalty and place it where it was before.

18. **FLATTENING AND REMOVING OBSTACLES.** You are not allowed to flatten the grass around your ball, either on the fairway or green or in the rough. You may lay your clubhead down in back of the ball (or in front of the ball with a putter) but you may not press down on the grass. In the rough, you may not trample the grass around the ball, but you can settle your feet to get a firm stance. Irregularities in the grass on the green may not be removed, but loose sticks or such may be removed. (See No. 19.) If you move your ball in removing a loose obstacle, this counts as a stroke. (In a friendly game this penalty may be waived.)

19. OBSTRUCTIONS. The definition of a "hazard" is important. Some obstructions on the course are meant to be hazards, but the following are *not* hazards; they may be removed or the ball may be removed from these and placed no nearer the green but in a clear space: any flagstick, guidepost, vehicle, implement, seat hut, shelter, bridge or plank, article of clothing, ground under repair, drain cover, hydrant, exposed water pipe, hole made by a greenskeeper, material piled for removal, pile of cut grass, wires, tree supports, electric light or telephone and telegraph poles, artificial steps, protective screens, ropes, stakes or railings, fountains, pumps, tanks, hoses, benches, tee boxes, ball-washers, bulletin boards, tents, refreshment stands, paper, bottles or similar objects. If the obstruction is movable it may be moved; if the object is not movable, your ball may be lifted and dropped not more than two club-lengths from the obstacle and not nearer the hole.

20. GROWING OBSTACLES. You may not move or break the branch of a tree or bush, or even bend it, except to enable you to get at your ball and take a proper stance and swing. You are not to improve the position of your ball by doing this.

21. DOUBLE HITS. You may not hit the ball twice with one stroke. This sometimes happens when you are putting, and it must be counted as two strokes.

22. BLOCKED BALL. When a ball not on the green is stymied (see No. 37) by another ball, the ball nearer the hole may be lifted upon request of either player involved, and then the lifted ball has to be replaced at the same spot.

23. BALL ON MOVE. If a ball lodges in a moving vehicle or anything moving, another ball must be dropped at the spot

where the vehicle was when the ball lodged in it. For instance, if a dog takes your ball, drop another near the spot. No penalty.

24. BALL ALTERED. If a ball in play but "at rest" is altered (such as being stepped on by a spectator and driven into the ground), then you may drop another ball. No penalty.

25. HIT BY BALL. If your ball hits you or your partner or caddie, you lose the hole (if you are playing match play) or take a two-stroke penalty (in stroke play).

26. WRONG BALL. If you play your opponent's ball by mistake, you lose the hole. But if he plays your ball before the mistake is discovered, there is no penalty for either of you, and you must play out the hole with the exchanged balls. If the mistake occurred through misinformation from a player or caddie, then there is no penalty in any case. If you play a ball belonging to someone outside your foursome and inform your party before the next player shoots, there is no penalty. But if you don't discover the mistake until later, then you lose the hole by forfeit.

27. SEARCHING. If your ball is found in deep rough, you may only remove enough of the rough so you can see the ball. The same holds true of a ball found in deep sand. If in searching for a ball, you accidentally kick it or move it, you may replace the ball at the spot where it was, without penalty.

28. LOST BALL. If your ball is lost or unplayable (see No. 29) you must drop a new ball as near as possible to the spot, and add a penalty stroke. If your ball was lost from the

tee, you may tee your next shot, and shoot again from the teeing area, adding a stroke.

29. PROVISIONAL BALL. If you think your ball has landed where it may be lost or unplayable, you may shoot a provisional ball (if played from the tee, wait till all the others in your party have shot), and then continue playing the provisional ball if your first is really lost. However, if you then find the first ball and it is playable, you must play that one, without penalty. You continue to play the provisional ball only until you reach the place where the first shot landed, then you search. The provisional ball (sometimes called a "mulligan") must be played before you go out and search, and before your caddie searches. You are the sole judge of whether your ball is unplayable—but it is definitely unplayable if it's in a water hazard or in "casual" water (see No. 34).

30. OUT-OF-BOUNDS. If your ball goes out-of-bounds, you must play your next shot from as near as possible to the same spot where you first shot, adding a penalty stroke for this (unless local rules say out-of-bounds loses distance only). If you played from the teeing area, you may tee up again. You may play a provisional ball (same as in No. 29) if you or your caddie thinks your ball has gone out-of-bounds. If you played from the tee, let the rest of your party shoot and then tee up and play the provisional ball. You may stand out-of-bounds to play a ball that is within bounds.

31. DAMAGED BALL. You may change a damaged ball if you tell your opponents you are doing so. You may *not* remove mud or in any way clean a ball while it is in play. Wait until you have holed out, and then wash the ball. (Sometimes this rule, with its penalty of two strokes for breaking it, is

waived in a friendly game.) However, if you lift your ball from a water hazard, casual water or ground under repair, you may clean it.

32. HAZARD PLAY. When playing a ball from a hazard (trap, bunker, running water, ditch, sand or road), you may not touch or move the ball while addressing it, and you must not even touch the ground with your club before you hit the ball! If there are loose steps in the hazard, you may remove them while you shoot. If there is any fixed obstruction (such as steps) in the hazard near your ball, you may move the ball not nearer the hole and place it in a similar position. You may smooth an irregularity, such as a footprint in a sand trap, for instance, provided it does not improve the lie of your ball. But you may not take your ball out of a footprint. You can see how important it is to fill up all holes in a bunker when you leave, so the next player doesn't land in your footprints. For the same reason, you should replace all divots on the fairway.

33. WATER HAZARDS. You may play a ball from moving water (such as a brook or lake) without penalty. If your ball lies or is lost in a recognized water hazard or in temporary ("casual") water *in a hazard* (such as in a sand trap), then you must take a penalty stroke and drop a ball behind the hazard, farther from the hole, or in another spot in the hazard. If you played the shot from the teeing area, you may shoot again from there, teeing up but counting the penalty stroke. In other words, if you drive from the tee into a lake, you count a penalty stroke and play your third shot from the tee.

34. CASUAL WATER. If your ball lands in "casual water" which has temporarily accumulated from rain, a hose, etc., but is not intended as a hazard, you may remove the ball

from the water, or if lost in the water play a new ball. You may play your next shot without penalty from dry ground as near as possible to the spot. The rule applies alike to "casual water" on fairway and green, or to a ball so near to "casual water" that you would have to take your stance in the water.

35. LINE OF PUTT. When there is a loose impediment on the putting green, you may remove it, but you may not remove it by pressing down with your club, and you may not remove it if it moves your ball. If your ball moves when you try, there is a penalty of one stroke. (Sometimes the penalty is waived in a friendly game.) You may not touch or press down the line of your putt, except by placing your putter blade in front of the ball while addressing it.

36. DIRECTING PUTT. Your partner, caddie or partner's caddie may tell you and point out the direction for putting, but may not touch the ground in advising you, or hold the pin or a club as a guide for you. No one may shield your putt from the wind. No one may scrape or rough the green to test it before putting. Don't putt until all other balls are at rest on the green.

37. STYMIES. The tournament rule for stymies is this: when a ball is within 6 inches (15 cm) of the hole or one ball is within 6 inches (15 cm) of the other, then the ball in the way may be lifted and replaced later in the same spot. For a ball to be laid stymie for you, it must be in the line of putt and more than 6 inches (15 cm) away from yours and also more than 6 inches (15 cm) from the hole. If you are stymied in a match, you must shoot over or around your opponent's ball. Medal play games (but not match play) waive the stymie rule and all balls in the line of putt are removed and replaced so each player has a clear line to putt; or else the ball nearer the hole is played

first. When a ball on the green is lifted the spot is marked by a coin. If the coin is in one's line of play, it must be moved a putter head length away, but no nearer the hole.

38. FLAGSTICK. The flagstick may be removed before you putt, if you request it. If you want the flagstick held by a caddie or player to mark the hole, you may request that. If the flagstick is left in the hole, and your ball rests against it, you are entitled to remove the stick and let the ball drop in the hole —if you can do it—without adding another stroke to your score. If your ball hits the flagstick when it is held by or has been removed by your partner or caddie, you technically lose the hole; if the stick is held by or has been removed by your opponent's side, they lose the hole. (This latter part is not usually adhered to in a friendly match.)

39. SINKING OPPONENT. In a match, if your ball knocks your opponent's ball into the hole, you have enabled him to hole out without his adding another stroke. In medal play this gives you a two-stroke penalty (often waived) and his ball must be replaced on the green.

40. PUTT HITS OPPONENT'S BALL. If you hit your opponent's ball with a putt, he may replace his ball if he prefers the original spot, but he must do this immediately before anyone else putts. If in hitting his ball, your ball stops on the same spot where his was, you must putt again before he replaces his. In medal play you must take a two-stroke penalty if your putt hits a competitor's ball, but this penalty is often waived in a friendly game.

41. LIP OF THE CUP. If you have holed out and your opponent's ball comes to rest on the lip of the cup, you may

knock his ball away conceding the next putt, and claim the hole if you are ahead, or announce the hole halved if his next stroke would tie you. If you do not knock away your opponent's ball, and it falls into the hole (from wind or vibration) your opponent is deemed to have holed out with his last putt. However, your opponent cannot stall to see if the ball drops, but must hole out without delay.

42. OUT OF TURN. For playing out of turn there is usually no penalty in a friendly game.

43. MATCH PLAY. In match play, the score is kept by holes. A hole is won by the player or side which holes the ball in fewer strokes. If both sides hole out in the same number of strokes, the hole is halved. A match consists of 18 holes, but if one player or side is two holes ahead with only one hole left to play, the match concludes on the 17th green. Likewise, the match may end on an earlier green if one side is ahead more holes than there are holes left to play in the 18.

44. MEDAL PLAY. In stroke ("medal") play, if two or more players end the round of 18 holes in a tie, they must play an extra hole or more than one until one or another player wins a hole, but the medal play rules apply to the extra holes, not match play.

45. CONCEDING PUTTS. You should not concede any putts in medal play, and in match play concede only those putts which stop on the lip of the cup (see No. 41).

46. EQUIPMENT. Use clubs and balls of standard specifications only. Shafts of putters may be fixed at any point in the head between the heel and the center of the sole, so some unusual-looking putters are perfectly legal.

47. TIME FOR SEARCHING. Technically speaking, a ball is lost if you can't find it within 5 minutes after the search has begun. You can give up a ball for lost before the 5 minutes are up, but you should not look longer.

These rules do not follow the same numbers as the official tournament rules of the U.S.G.A. and the R. & A., but they are more or less in the same sequence. Refer to them whenever you need to, remember the main points, and follow them in general to keep your friendly game friendly!

Appendix

ADDRESS A golfer has addressed his ball as soon as he has taken his stance and grounded his club behind the ball. In a hazard, where it is not permitted to ground the club, taking a stance constitutes the address.

ADVICE Any suggestion which could influence a golfer in making up his mind how to play, what club to use or the method of playing a stroke is advice. It can be sought or accepted only from a player's partner or either of their caddies. Information on rules or local rules is not advice, nor is information about the line of play for a hole.

ALBATROSS A score of three below the par for a hole.

ATTENDING THE FLAG A player is entitled to have the flag attended and held up to indicate the position of the hole at any time. On the green it is an infringement for a ball (played from on the green) to strike an unattended flagstick.

BACKSPIN See *PITCH*.

BEST BALL A match in which one player competes against the best ball of two or three other players.

BIRDIE A score of one below the par for a hole.

BLASTER A broad-soled wedge.

BOGEY A score of one more than the par for a hole. Thus double-bogey, triple-bogey, etc.

BRASSIE Old term for 2-wood.

BUNKER Hazard consisting of an area of bare earth, or sand, usually in the form of a depression. Grass banks and artificial walls of bunkers are not part of the hazard.

CADDIE A person employed to carry a player's clubs and offer advice. Players are responsible for the actions of their caddies and suffer penalties for any infringement of rules by their caddies.

CASUAL WATER Any temporary accumulation of water which is clearly visible after the player has taken his stance. Snow and ice may be treated as casual water or loose impediments at the discretion of the player.

CHIP A low, running shot played from just off the green.

CLEEK Obsolescent term for 4-wood.

COMPETITOR Player in a stroke-play competition. A fellow competitor is a player he accompanies during play and may be his marker. A fellow competitor is not a partner within the rules.

DIVOT A slice of turf displaced in making a shot. It is one of the canons of golf etiquette that divots should be replaced and firmly trodden into position.

DORMIE, DORMY A player (or side) is said to be dormie when he is as many holes up in the match as there are holes left to be played and he therefore cannot be beaten. The expression is believed to derive from the French verb *dormir* (to sleep) since the player can go to sleep and still not be beaten.

DRAW An intentional stroke which causes the ball to move in a controlled manner from right to left through the air.

DRIVING IRON 1-iron.

DUBBED SHOT A badly hit shot.

DUFFER A beginning golfer.

EAGLE A score of two under the par of a hole.

EQUIPMENT Anything used, worn or carried by a player or his caddie, including golf carts, but not his ball in play.

FADE An intentional stroke which causes the ball to move from left to right through the air in a controlled manner.

FAIRWAY The mown portion of the playing area of a course between the tee and green. The rules of golf do not distinguish between fairways and rough (although special local rules may).

FAT A golfer is said to have hit the ball "fat" when his club-head contacts the ground before striking the ball. Also used to describe the heart of the green—for example: "I ignored the flag and aimed for the fat of the green."

FAULTLESS PLAY Completing a hole in the number of strokes assigned to that hole (par).

FLAGSTICK Movable indicator to mark the position of a hole. Colloquially referred to as pin, flag or stick.

FLEX The amount of spring or resilience in the shaft.

FLYER A ball hit out of control.

FORE! Conventional golfer's cry to warn players ahead of an approaching ball.

FORECADDIE A person employed by a competition committee to mark the landing of golf balls, especially on blind holes and in areas of excessive rough.

FOUR-BALL A match in which two players play their better ball against the better ball of two other partners.

FOURSOME The most players who can play a round together is four and the group is called a foursome.

GRAIN OF THE GREEN The direction in which the grass is growing. If you see a shine, the grass is growing away from you, and you will be putting with the grain. If you see no shine, you are putting against the grain and you must use a little extra effort to make your putt reach the cup.

GREEN The prepared putting surface. A ball is on the green when any part of it touches the green.

GROUND UNDER REPAIR Any part of the course marked as such by the committee; material piled for removal.

HALF A hole completed in the same net scores by both sides in match play is said to result in a half, or to be halved. Also used in the same sense to describe the result of a drawn match.

HANGING LIE A lie on sloping ground which forces the golfer to play from an uneven stance.

HAZARD Any bunker or water hazard defined as such by the committee.

HOLE The hole is standardized at 4.2 inches in diameter (106 mm) and at least 4 inches (100 mm) deep. If a liner is used it must be sunk at least 1 inch (25 mm) below the surface.

HOLED A ball is judged to be holed when all of it lies within the circumference of the hole and below the lip.

HONOR The privilege of playing first from the tee.

HOOK An unintentional stroke which causes the ball to fly from right to left through the air in an uncontrolled manner.

LINE OF PLAY Usually abbreviated to "the line," as in "What is the line on this hole?" Means the preferred route.

LINKS Another term for a golf course of any kind.

LOCAL RULES Rules formulated by local committees to cover special conditions on the course.

LOFT The angle by which a clubface is set back from the perpendicular.

LOOSE IMPEDIMENTS Natural objects, not fixed or growing. Includes stones if not firmly embedded, fallen twigs and leaves, dung, worms and insects, and casts made by them. Sand and loose soil are classified as loose impediments on the green but not through the green. Snow and ice may be classified as loose impediments or casual water, at the discretion of the player.

LOST BALL A ball is declared to be lost if it is not found within 5 minutes; or if the owner puts another ball into play; or if the player formally abandons his ball, whether or not he searches for it; or if he plays any stroke with a provisional ball beyond the place where the original ball was likely to be.

MARKER A person, often a fellow competitor, charged with keeping a competitor's score. It is, however, the responsibility of the player to ensure the accuracy of his score.

MATCH PLAY The form of golf which is contested on the number of holes won, rather than by the total number of strokes taken for a round (stroke play). Special rules operate for match play golf.

MEDAL PLAY Stroke play.

MIDIRON 2-iron.

MOVED BALL A ball is judged to have moved if it comes to rest in another position. Rocking, or oscillation, does not count as movement for purposes of penalty at the address provided the ball settles back into its original position.

MULLIGAN (see *PROVISIONAL BALL*) The practice, quite unofficial, of allowing a player a "free" second drive when his first shot is unsatisfactory.

NAP Sometimes called grain. It is the texture of a putting surface caused by grasses tending to lie in the same direction.

OBSERVER A person appointed by the committee to help a referee decide questions of fact and report any infringements.

OBSTRUCTION Anything artificial erected, placed or left on the course, except boundary fences, walls and stakes and artificial roads and paths. The committee may decree any such to be an

123

integral part of the course in which case the rules for relief from obstructions do not apply.

OUT-OF-BOUNDS A ball is out-of-bounds when all of it lies over a line drawn between the nearest inside points of boundary stakes. If a line is used to define a boundary the line itself is out-of-bounds.

OUTSIDE AGENCY Any agency not part of the match. In stroke play outside agencies include referees, markers, fellow competitors and observers.

PAR The norm for a hole. In most countries par is set exclusively on length. Holes up to 250 yards (225 m) are par-3; 251–475 yards (226–428 m) are par-4; 476 yards (429 m) and over are par-5.

PARTNER A player on the same side.

PENALTY A stroke, or strokes, to be added to the score under the rules. Penalty strokes do not affect the order of play in foursomes.

PIN HIGH A shot finishing level with the flagstick is said to be pin high, and therefore a perfect length but not necessarily straight.

PITCH A high, arching shot. Normally used to describe such shots played to a green.

PRESS The act of spoiling a shot by hitting too hard.

PROVISIONAL BALL A ball played in place of a ball which is lost, or out-of-bounds, or unplayable.

PULL An unintentional shot which flies in a straight line to the left of the target.

PUSH Opposite of pull. In this case the ball goes in a straight line right of target.

PUTT A stroke played on the green with a putter.

REFEREE A person appointed by a committee to accompany players and rule on questions of fact and golf law. His decision is final.

ROUGH Area along each fairway which consists of fairly low grass for a 6-foot (2-m) width, and beyond this, high or deep rough which can be as wide and as rough as any uncultivated landscape.

ROUND ROBIN A type of match play competition in which every entrant plays against everyone else, the person with the most victories being the winner.

RUBBER CORE A ball made by winding rubber thread under tension around a central core and then covering with a plastic casing. This is the universal method of manufacturing the highest grade balls.

RUB OF THE GREEN The expression to cover the case of a moving ball being stopped or deflected by an outside agency. Commonly it is used to describe any piece of golfing luck, good or bad, for which there is no provision in the rules.

SAND WEDGE Specialist club for playing recovery shot from sand.

SHANK A stroke in which the neck of the club makes contact with the ball, sending it off at an acute angle.

SLICE Unintentional shot which causes the ball to veer from left to right in an uncontrolled manner through the air.

SOLE THE PUTTER To place the putter blade in front of the ball, sight along the imaginary path you want the putt to follow, and finally bring the putter back in back of the ball, in position for the swing.

SPOON Obsolescent term for 3-wood.

STANCE The placing of the feet in position in preparation for making a stroke. A stance is not necessarily an address.

STROKE A forward movement of the club made with the intention of fairly striking the ball.

STROKE PLAY Also known as medal play. The system of golf in which a player counts his total of strokes for a round.

STYMIE A ball lying in the line of putt and more than 6 inches (15 cm) away from yours and also more than 6 inches (15 cm) from the hole.

TEE A peg for teeing the ball or the prepared area on which the teeing-ground is sited.

TEE (TEEING-GROUND) A rectangle two club-lengths in depth measured back from a line between the markers.

TEXAS WEDGE A shot played from off the green with a putter.

THREE-BALL A match in which three players each play against the two others.

THREESOME A group of three playing together.

TOP The action of striking the ball's top half, producing a low, scuttling shot.

TRAP A bunker or sand hazard.

WAGGLE Preliminary movement of the club at address before making a stroke.

WEDGE Broad-soled club designed for pitching.
WHIFF THE BALL To miss the ball.
WINTER RULES Special local rules employed by committees to protect the course in winter. Conventions vary from club to club and players should always check the local rules to determine the type and degree of relief which is permissible.

Photo by Franklin Berger

QUESTIONS TO ASK IN PICKING A GOLF SCHOOL

[This section courtesy *Golf Digest*, April, 1976,
© Golf Digest Inc.]

An improved game is the sole objective for most persons attending a golf school. To reach this goal, a student must come away with an understanding of how the correct swing works. Since it takes a bit more than loose change to "matriculate" at a golf school, prospective enrollees should make a serious evaluation of the facility they are considering.

Every spring *Golf Digest* publishes a list of golf schools and camps. No evaluation of the schools is offered. But in preparing the list and visiting a number of schools, these guidelines become apparent:

1. Instructors

Investigate the reputation of the instructors. Are they good teachers? Have they had ample experience in teaching golf? Don't take the school's word for these important factors. Contact golf association officials who may be familiar with the teachers. If all else fails, ask the school administrators where the professionals have worked, or are working. Club members will give you an honest appraisal of their professional.

If the school has a "name" professional on its teaching staff—a tournament star, for instance—try to find out how long he or she will actually be on hand. In the past, at least, some schools have enrolled students who expect to be taught by a tournament star, then find that such a personality actually has little or perhaps no time to appear in person. Also, some successful tournament stars may have no actual teaching experience.

2. Program

Find out about the details of the teaching program. Make certain that aspects of golf other than the full swing are taken into consideration—i.e., trouble shots, bunker play, chipping, putting. It won't do you much good to be able to hit the ball a long way if you can't putt.

In this regard, strategy—golf course management—should play an important part in the teaching program. Sometimes good management alone can take several strokes off your game.

127

3. Individual vs. clinical instruction

Top grade schools are heavy on individual instruction, the one-on-one approach. Of course, it isn't possible to have one instructor teach one student for the entire session. Yet, clinics should take up less than a quarter of the time. As a student, you should be under the observation of an instructor 100 per cent of the time. This would include individual and clinical instruction plus playing lessons.

4. Teaching consistency

Every instructor at the school should teach the same method. It would be confusing if the instructors had different ideas about the golf swing.

5. Visual aids

Visual aids could include photography, diagrams of golfing set-ups and alignment, video tapes, movies, etc. Instructors who employ visual aids are usually more effective.

6. Follow-up

What does the school give you to take home? A personalized notebook, with the instructors' own notes on your strong swing points, your weaknesses and how to cure them, and your own notes, is a valuable post-school aid. It's something you can refer to should your swing go sour. Some schools offer movies of your swing—when you first come and when you finish. Combining your own notebook and movies of your swing makes sense.

7. Case histories

Reputable schools will provide prospective students with "case histories" of former pupils whose swings and games improved after a session. The school, upon request, should provide you with addresses of such students. You could question them by telephone or mail. If you suspect "plants"—former students who may have been paid to say nice things about the school—ask for names of others who have attended. Then ask these golfers how the school impressed them.

8. Facilities

The practice area is probably the most important physical facility. That's where you'll be spending much of your time as a student. Practice bunkers, chipping areas and greens are a must. A well-conditioned course that is strong enough to put up a fight is essential. That's where you'll be learning course management.

9. Climate

The normal climate at the school's location at the time you want to attend is important. Any area that doesn't have an average daily temperature history of at least 60°F (16°C) for the period you plan to be there ought to be checked off. It's tough to concentrate on golf when your teeth are chattering.

10. Food and lodging

Creature comforts are more important to some than others. Adequate lodging should be a requirement; good food, a place to relax—maybe even a beach.

All of the listed guidelines also apply to golf camps for teen-age boys and girls. In addition, there are a few other items to consider.

Most younger people want other activities along with golf. Swimming, tennis, game rooms, short trips to nearby places of interest, amusements, movies—things like that. Sure, they want to learn to play golf, but they aren't old enough to make it a life-and-death matter like the rest of us!

Parents want to be assured there is plenty of adult supervision, both during the golf lessons and at the evening activities.

Most youngsters aren't quite as demanding as their parents about creature comforts, but it wouldn't hurt to check out the meal situation.

One thing about golf schools—good ones represent an unequalled opportunity to learn. If you go, don't waste your time sniffing the roses. You can do that on your own, later.

—John P. May

U.S. GOLF SCHOOL DIRECTORY

School	Costs	Particulars
	(Latest information)	
Arnold Palmer Golf Academy 6200 Bay Hill Rd. Orlando, FL. 32811	Four 2-week sessions beginning in July. $550. 2nd year	Boys only, 11–17. Play 27-hole Bay Hill Course. Palmer appears at each session. Resort. Disney World nearby.
Billy Casper's California Golf Camp 8245 Ronson Road San Diego, CA 92111	Two 2-week sessions beginning 7/2, 7/23; two 3-week sessions beginning 7/2, 7/23. $625.(2 weeks), $885.(3 weeks). 6th year.	Coed, 10–18. Limit 50. Play at top San Diego courses. Casper attends each session. College dorms.
Billy Casper's Northern California Golf Camp. 8245 Ronson Road San Diego, CA 92111	One 2-week session beginning 7/2; one 3-week session beginning 7/2. $625.(2 weeks), $885.(3 weeks). 4th year.	Coed, 10–18. Limit 50. At Lake Shastina. Casper attends each session. College dorms.
Boyne Natl. Golf Academy P.O. Box 72 Boyne Falls, Mich. 49713	One 2-week session beginning 6/19. $475. 10th year.	Coed, 10–16. Play 2 18-hole courses. Pro instruction. Resort facilities.
Camp Penn Hall 4591 Old Frankstown Rd. Monroeville, Pa. 15146	Two 1-week sessions beginning 6/19. $140. ($250. 2 weeks). 13th year.	Boys only, 10–17. Play 5 area courses. Charles Deasy, dir. Indoor fieldhouse. Dorms.

Challenge Golf Academy P.O. Box 11658, 235 Atlas Bldg. Salt Lake City, Utah 84101	Two 1-week sessions beginning 6/20. $450. 7th year.	Adults, coed 10 and over. Play Park City course. Ben Doyle, dir. Resort.
Chase Golf Camp Bethlehem, N.H. 03574 winter mailing address: Box 1446 Manchester, Mass. 01944	Two 4-week sessions beginning 6/24, 7/26. Two 2-week sessions beginning 7/26, 8/10. $840. ($420. 2 weeks). 11th year.	Coed, 11–17. Limit 75. 18-hole Championship course, par-6 hole, 9-hole par-3 course. Sam Patton heads program. Professional staff. Evening activities program. Recreational activities. Dorms. (Resort adult instruction—write for info.)
Clauson's Golf School & Caddie Camp Hatchville, Mass. 02536	10-week session beginning 6/23. $650. ($400. 5 weeks). 15th year.	Boys only, 11–16. Play Clauson 18-hole course. 5 pros instruct. Cabins.
Crimson Tide Sports Academy Box K Univ. of Alabama University, Ala. 35486	Four 1-week sessions beginning in June. $175. 7th year.	Coed, 10–17. Limit 40. Play at Univ. course. Coach Conrad Rehling. College dorms.
Duke University Youth Golf Camp Duke Golf Course Durham, N.C. 27706	Three 1-week sessions beginning 6/18, 6/25, 7/9. $225. ($420. 2 weeks). 5th year.	Boys only, 6/18, 6/25; girls only, 7/9. 11–18. Limit 70. Rod Myers, dir., other pros. 18-hole Championship course. College dorms. Swimming.
Ferris State Golf Camp Katke Golf Course Ferris State College Big Rapids, Mich. 49307	Two sessions, 7/23–7/28 & 7/30–8/4. $150. ($75. Day students). 4th year.	Coed, 10–17. Limit 25. Play 18-hole course. Norm Bennett, dir. PGA pros. Additional activities. College dorms.

Florida PGA Section Golf Acad. c/o Roger Ganem 4381 Sanderling Circle East Quail Ridge 725 Boynton Beach, FL 33436	One session, 6/18–6/23. $195. 3rd year.	Coed, 10–17. Play at Mission Inn 18-hole Championship course. Douglas MacArthur, dir. Pros. Resort facilities.
Foxfire Golfswing Program Box 711 Pinehurst, N.C. 28374.	Three 1-week sessions beginning 6/18, 6/25, 7/9. $325. 9th year.	Coed, 9–20. Limit 20. 27-hole course. Paul Bertholy, dir. (Adult instruction—write for info.)
Golf Academy of the Southwest c/o Johnson A. King 3811 Country Lane Conroe, Texas 77302	One session, 6/11–6/16. $247. 3rd year.	Coed, 13–17. Limit 35. Play at Waterwood Natl. course. West Hilzer, dir. Pros. Additional activities.
Harder Hall Golf & Tennis Camps Harder Hall Sebring, FL 33870	One-week sessions beginning 6/28, 7/12, 7/19, 7/26, 8/2, 8/9. $265. week ($1025. 4 wks., $1225. 5 wks., $1425. 6 wks., $1600. 7 wks.) 13th year.	Coed, 12–17. Play Championship 18-hole course at resort. Doug Ford, Jr., other pros. Evening activities; recreational activities.
Johnny Miller New England Golf Academy 24 Woods Ave. Worcester, Mass. 01606	One 3-week session beginning 7/24. $875. 1st year.	Coed, 10–18. Play at Nichols College course. Glen Albaugh, dir. Miller appears. Dorms.
Morehead State Univ. Golf Camp c/o Rex Chaney Morehead State Univ. Box 864 Morehead, KY 40351	One session, 6/25–6/30. $110. 7th year.	Coed, 10–18. Limit 40. Rex Chaney, dir. Additional activities. College dorms.

Maryland Golf Camp Univ. of Maryland Golf Course College Park, MD. 20742	Two sessions, 6/26-6/30 & 7/24-7/28. $100. 7th year.	Coed, 10-18. Limit 40. Day camp only (no lodging). Frank Cronin, dir. Pros on staff.
Natl. Academy of Golf, PGA of America Box 12458 Lake Park, FL 33403	Three 1-week sessions beginning 6/18, 6/25, 7/9. $295. 2nd year.	Coed, 12-17, for better players. Limit 60. Play at 54-hole Boca West Complex. Gary Wiren, dir. Pros on staff.
NEPGA Golf Camp & School c/o George Wemyss P.O. Box 81 Wakefield, Mass. 01880	One session, 6/25-6/30. $110. 2nd year.	Boys only, 12-17. Limit 60. Play 18-hole course at Canton, Mass. Revolving staff of pros.
No. Texas Golf Academy 2815 Valley View Lane Suite 214 Dallas, TX 75245	Four 1-week sessions beginning 6/11, 6/18, 6/25, 7/9. $230.	Boys only except last session coed, 12-17. Limit 50. Pros. Dorms.
Paul Harney Golf Academy 74 Club Valley Drive East Falmouth, MA 02536	Three-day session, write for dates. $150. Day school. $185-$250. Overnight school.	Coed, 10-18. Play 18-hole course. Harney appears daily.
Peggy Kirk Bell Youth Golfari Pine Needles Lodges & C.C. Box 88 So. Pines, N.C. 28387	One 2-week session, 7/2-7/15. $660. 9th year.	Coed, 10-18. Limit 80. Play at Pine Needles. Staff headed by Bell; additional pros. Resort facilities. (Adult instruction—write for info.)
Pinehurst School of Golf Pinehurst Country Club Box 4000 Pinehurst, N.C. 28374	Six 1-week sessions beginning 6/11. $295. 12th year.	Boys only except girls only 7/2, 11-17. Play championship golf course. Lou Miller, dir.; other pros. Additional activities.
Princeton Hills Golf Academy 700 Park Ave. Plainfield, N.J. 07060	Nine 1-week sessions beginning 6/19. $235. 9th year.	Coed, 12-18. Lawrenceville School course. Art Silvestrone, pro. Dorms.

Silver Sands Jr. Golf Academy 1809 S. Shore Drive Delavan, Wis. 53115	Eight 1-week sessions beginning 6/11 $205. ($390. 2 weeks). 4th year.	Boys only, 10-17. Limit 25-30. Play 18-hole championship course. Wayne Rolfs, dir. Pros. Lakeside resort. Additional activities.
Soaring Eagles Golf Camp Elmira College Elmira, N.Y. 14901	Eight 1-week sessions beginning 6/19. $215. 8th year.	Coed, 9-17. 18-hole course. Paul Cornelius, dir. Dorms.
So. Calif. PGA Jr. Golf Camp Stardust C.C. San Diego, CA 92110	One 4-day session, 8/2-8/5. $65. Days only.	Coed, 12-17. Limit 80. Cliff Crandall, dir. 18-hole course.
Tennessee Golf Academy Box 50574 Nashville, Tenn. 37205	Four 1-week sessions beginning 6/11, 6/18, 7/16, 7/23. $188. 6th year.	Boys only, 11-17. Limit 50. Tenn. PGA conducts. Pros. 18-hole championship course. Lodge. Swimming.
Texas A & M Golf School Texas A & M Univ. College Station, TX 77843	One 12-day session, 7/9-7/21. $400. 4th year.	Boys only, 13-16. Limit 30. Coach Bob Ellis conducts; other pros on staff daily. Play 18-hole course. Swimming. Dorms.
West Coast Golf Academy 19251 Portos Dr. Saratoga, CA. 95070	1-week session beginning 6/19. $215. 7th year.	Boys only, 10-18. Play 18-hole course. Roger Swanson, dir. Cottages.
Whispering Pines Golf School Whispering Pines, N.C. 28389	Four 1-week sessions beginning 7/17. $235. 13th year.	Boys only, 11-17. Play 4 18-hole courses. Pete Piestrak, dir. Resort lodgings, facilities. Golfers should bring own

* Costs and enrollment limits are for one session, and with noted exceptions include room, board, instruction, etc., while at camp. Taxes, gratuities may be extra. None includes transportation. Golfers should bring own clubs and golf shoes.

SAMPLE GOLF SCHOOL PROGRAM

Following is a recent example of the type of program offered by golf schools in the U.S. As in the directory to schools which starts on page 130, dates and fees may change yearly and the school should be contacted in advance for present particulars.

PGA NATIONAL ACADEMY OF GOLF—Junior Level PGA of America
Box 12458
Lake Park, Florida 33403
AN OPPORTUNITY TO LEARN ● A PLACE TO MAKE
    FRIENDS ● A TIME TO HAVE FUN

PGA National Academy of Golf

An important objective of the PGA of America is advancement of the game of golf. Key to such progress is player development, and the PGA National Academy of Golf makes a significant contribution to that development. This summer the Academy will focus on the Junior level with a program designed for 120 intermediate and advanced boys and girls between the ages of 12 and 17. Junior golfers will have an opportunity to learn from the best in the PGA National Academy of Golf. Set for three 1-week sessions, the Academy offers instruction by past PGA National Champions, current Tour stars and leading PGA Club Professionals.

FOR BOYS & GIRLS

Facilities

Instruction and playing will be at the 54-hole Boca West golf complex in Boca Raton, Florida.

The complex has three top calibre eighteen hole golf courses plus an ample practice range for individual and group instruction.

Lodging

Housing facilities will be at St. Andrew's School, half a mile from the golf complex. There are dorm facilities for boys and girls and various forms of recreation, such as swimming pools, tennis courts and a student lounge. All meals will be prepared and served on the Campus grounds.

Training

Students will receive individual instruction, both on the practice tee and on the golf course, in addition to group clinics and competition.

The week-long schedule will include course strategy, tournament activity, team competition, classroom lectures and movies on Rules, Etiquette and History of the game and recreational free time, all under the supervision of PGA Golf Professionals.

Students will benefit from the PGA's premier use of electronic equipment including video tape machines and the Mitchell stop-action camera.

Juniors will be tested on a Golf Swing Analyzer which measures clubhead speed, path and alignment, as well as flight path and carry distance, thus giving better understanding of the principles of the golf swing through instant feedback on their progress.

Maximum enrollment per session will be 60 students, so please indicate first and second choices on the application form.

The tuition of $_____ covers all instruction, room, board (3 meals per day) range and green fees for the entire session and is payable at the time of application.

Refunds, less a processing fee of $____, will be made upon written request PRIOR TO JUNE – , 19– .

PGA Club Professionals

BOB ROSS
Pinetree Golf Club
Delray Beach, Fla.
LAURIE HAMMER
Delray Dunes
Golf & Country Club
Boynton Beach, Fla.
ROGER KENNEDY
Pompano Beach Golf Club
Pompano, Fla.
CARMEN CEO
Frenchmen's Creek
Golf & Country Club
North Palm Beach, Fla.

MICKIE GALLAGHER
Atlantis Golf Club
Atlantis, Fla.
ED MITCHELL
Bonaventure Country Club
Ft. Lauderdale, Fla.
RON POLANE
Boca Raton Hotel & Club
Boca Raton, Fla.
DR. GARY WIREN
Director
PGA National Academy
of Golf

JOHN GERRING
Holly Tree Country Club
Simpsonville, S.C.

JOHN ZUREK *Coordinator*
PGA National Academy
of Golf

PGA Staff and Consultants to the Academy (partial list)

JULIUS BOROS
JAY HEBERT
TOM WATSON
TOM KITE

HALE IRWIN
STEVE MELNYK
ANDY NORTH
JIM SIMONS

SAMPLE SCHOLARSHIP

FRANCIS OUIMET CADDIE SCHOLARSHIP FUND
190 *Park Road, Weston, Mass.* 02193

BASIC REQUIREMENTS:
  Proven leadership, character, integrity.
  Evaluation of academic achievement and potential.
  Minimum of 3 years full time service to golf in Massachusetts.
  Plans to attend an accredited institution of undergraduate
    higher education.
  Clearly establish need of scholarship aid.
CANDIDATES:
  Candidates should apply in writing mid-summer of or early in
    their senior year in high school.
DEADLINE:
  Deadline is December 1st of the year preceding the request for
    scholarship aid.
CONTACT:
  Please contact the Executive Director, Ouimet Fund, Ouimet
    Museum/Golf House, 190 Park Road, Weston, Mass. 02193.
    Phone: (617) 891–6400.

PGA APPRENTICE PROGRAM

For those young golfers who are seriously considering making golfing their career, an Apprentice Program has been established to prepare prospective members for membership in the Professional Golfers' Association of America, and in so doing provides the best possible foundation to produce qualified golf professionals. The Program is designed to raise the standards of prospective members through involvement, education, motivation and communication.

A very brief outline of the Program follows. For full details, contact the PGA, Box 12458, Lake Park, Florida 33403.

WHAT APPRENTICESHIP MEANS: Registration and participation in the Program means that a registrant is pursuing membership as a "prospective member" through eligible, full-time employment in the golf profession as the major occupation.

ELIGIBILITY: An applicant must be employed in the golf profession on a full-time basis. All employment must be within a Section of the PGA of America. An applicant must be at least 18 years of age at the time he applies for apprentice status.

FEES: $30 initial "one-time" only fee, plus additional insurance fees.

CREDITS AND MONTHS: All prospective members must accumulate 32 experience credits and 40 months in the golf profession in order to fulfill their time requirements for membership. An apprentice accumulates months for each month he remains active in the Apprentice Program. An apprentice accumulates credits for each month he is employed and working at his course. Normally credits towards membership may not be gained while a person is still a high school student. Experience may be cumulative over a period of years, but no experience may be counted unless it is on a full-time basis and unless the person claiming such experience is engaged in the golf profession as a major occupation at the time the experience is gained. The applicant will have a maximum of 6 years from the date of initial registration to fulfill the requirements and apply for membership.

PGA BUSINESS SCHOOLS: The satisfactory completion of these Schools is mandatory for membership in the PGA of America. The Schools are conducted as a series which begins in the fall of one year and extends through the spring of the following year.

SAMPLE JUNIOR TOURNAMENT
PGA National Junior Championship
Finals at Callaway Gardens, Pine Mt., Georgia

Conditions of Entry:
Contestants will consist of boys and girls up through the age of 17 (no minimum age limit).

Play will be governed by the Rules of Golf and Amateur Status as approved by the USGA.

Application for entry is subject to acceptance and, if accepted, may be rejected or revoked at any time thereafter by the PGA Junior Golf Tournament Committee acting in behalf of the Professional Golfers' Association of America and the PGA Corporation, for any reason deemed good cause by the Committee at its discretion, without liability to the Committee, Association, or Corporation, or the sponsors of the tournament.

The Committee reserves the right to adjust dates, format and other details to fit conditions prevailing at the time of the tournaments.

FOR INFORMATION ON DATES, ETC., CALL: (305) 848–3481

Entry Regulations
(Contestant and Parent Must Read Before Signing)

All entries must be filed on the Official Entry Form procured at a local PGA Golf Shop.

Contestant must have his playing ability or handicap verified by a PGA golf professional.

Completed Entry Form must be sent to PGA National Junior Championship, P.O. Box 14456, North Palm Beach, Florida 33403.

$5.00 entry fee (check or money order made out to PGA of America) must accompany entry.

Deadlines of Entries for Local Qualifying:
Completed entries must be in PGA Headquarters no later than June — .

Incomplete applications or applications received after this date will not be accepted. Date of postmark will not be considered.

INFORMATION FOR WOMEN GOLFERS

The Women's Metropolitan Golf Association offers a special Junior membership to any girl living in the Greater New York metropolitan area (New Jersey, Long Island, Connecticut and Westchester) who has not reached her 18th birthday. This special program is comprised of a Championship, the Maureen Orcutt Medal Tournament, a mixed tournament with boys under the age of 18, and an Inter-City Team Match against Philadelphia and Boston.

The first organized Junior Girls competition in golf in the United States was sponsored by the W.M.G.A. in 1921, and throughout the years it has boasted such prominent names among junior champions as: Helen Hicks, Cookie Swift, Judy Frank, Judy Cooperstein and Cindy Ferro.

Each of the three metropolitan districts has a caddie-scholarship fund.

The Colgate-Palmolive Company annually awards a scholarship to a young woman golfer based on academic excellence, golfing ability and financial need.

FOR INFORMATION, contact:
Women's Metropolitan Golf Association, Inc.
310 Lexington Ave.
New York, N.Y. 10016

INDEX

141